CLIL

Content & Language Integrated Learning

Writing about Global Relations

Paul Underwood

Miyako Nakaya

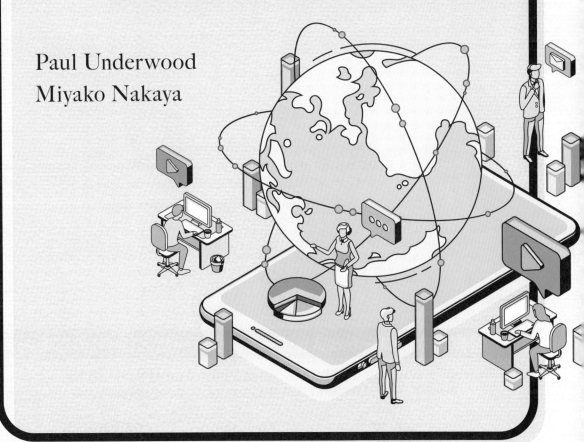

SANSHUSHA

図版出典

Unit 7: https://www.un.org/sustainabledevelopment/
         The content of this publication has not been approved
         by the United Nations and does not reflect the views of
         the United Nations or its officials or Member States.
Unit 9: naum/shutterstock
Unit 10: gmast3r/iStockphoto
Unit 12: anttohoho/iStockphoto
Unit 14: GoodIdeas/shutterstock

音声ダウンロード＆ストリーミングサービス（無料）のご案内

https://www.sanshusha.co.jp/text/onsei/isbn/9784384335255/

本書の音声データは、上記アドレスよりダウンロードおよびストリーミング再生ができます。ぜひご利用ください。

Download

Streaming

(Disc1-1) の表示は教室用 CD のディスク番号とトラック番号です。

1))) マークは、「音声ダウンロード＆ストリーミングサービス」での MP3 ファイル番号です。

はじめに

　このテキストは、CLIL（Content and Language Integrated Learning）の指導法を元に作られています。Content の部分で、国際関係の基礎や国際問題に関して学習し、Language の部分は、その内容についてのインタラクティブなタスクを実施しスピーキング力をつけ、ゴールとして、パラグラフやエッセイの構造を学習し、内容について考えをまとめ、ライティング力をつけるというものです。

　従来のライティングのテキストでは、「書き方」が中心でした。さらに、内容に関し、1つのテーマに絞ると、使い手である学習者の専攻が限定されてしまうという難しさがありました。しかしこの国際関係の基礎や国際問題を学ぶことは、グローバリゼーションの世の中、どの専攻の学生にも、今世界で起こっていることを考える手助けになります。このテキストでは、1つ1つのトピックを厳選し、全体で首尾一貫したテーマを提供できるように考えられています。

　また、このテキストは、英語と日本語と両方で学ぶスタイルになっています。この2つの言語を使用し、国際関係の基礎や国際問題を学び、かつ英語の力もつけるという、2つのゴールを目指しています。

各ユニットの構成

Can Do	その課の目標を確認します。
Type and structure	パラグラフやエッセイの構造について学びます。
Content	国際関係についての知識を身につけ、ペアやグループワークを通してアクティブラーニングを実践します。
Writing task	その課のテーマに沿ったパラグラフやエッセイを書きます。
Grammar for writing	その課のパラグラフやエッセイを書く時に必要な語彙や文法事項を確認します。

　ほんとうの意味でのCLILのライティング教科書を味わってください。

　また、この新しい試みを許可してくださった三修社編集部の永尾真理氏、具体的な内容構成の形を率先して提案してくださった菊池暁氏に感謝申し上げます。

Paul Underwood／仲谷　都

Contents

Contentを学習するとき、ペアやグループで使うフレーズです。それぞれのユニットで必要な箇所にこのページが書いてあります。ここに戻って来て見てください。

LANGUAGE FOR LEARNING

"What did you get [for Number 1]?"

"I got [   ]. How about you?"

"I wrote [   ]."

"What does ～ mean (in Japanese)?"

"What's another word for ～ ?"

"Does [   ] mean ～ in Japanese?"

"How do you spell that?"

"Could you explain that again?"

"Could you say that again / the last part, again?"

"Could you speak more slowly, please?"

"Could you repeat that / the first part / the last part, please?"

"I think it's 'True' because it says in the passage that ～ "

"[Maiko], what do you think?"

"What did you think about ['A']?"

"I think it describes [liberal / realist / both]. How about you?"

"I think [   ]."

"Let's ask the teacher for help."

DISCUSSION PHRASES

"What do you think ～ ?"

"What are your thoughts [about ～]?"

"[Harry,]do you agree with [Tom]?"

"I see what you mean, but I think ～ "

"Could you give an example?"

"That's a good point."

"That's a good suggestion."

"I agree with [Yuki] [about ～]." / "Yes, I think [Yuki] is right [about ～]."

"I somewhat agree [, but I also think ～]."

"I'm sorry, but I don't agree [about ～ / on that point]."

Unit 1 — Learning about global relations

Can Do
Structure: パラグラフと3つの構成部分について知る。
Content: なぜ国際関係の基礎を知るべきか、考える。

S: パラグラフの構成部分を学びます。

C: 日々、さまざまなことが世界各地で起こっています。この時代に国と国との関係を理解する重要性について確認しましょう。

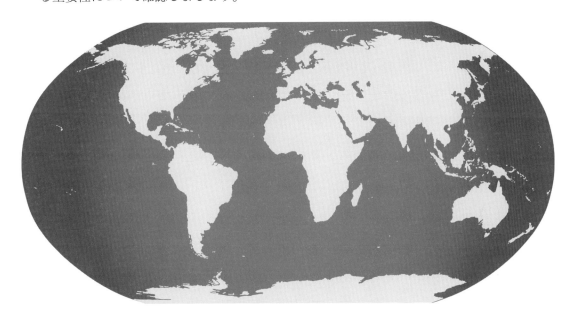

I The Organization of an English Paragraph

A) パラグラフって何?

1つずつの単語がいくつか集まって文を作り、文がいくつか集まって、1つのパラグラフを作ります。そのパラグラフがいくつか集まったものを、エッセイと呼び、そのエッセイがいくつか集まったものが一冊の本になります。

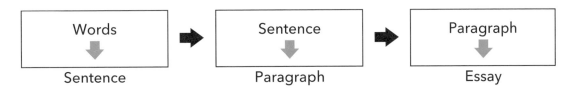

B) パラグラフの構成部分

1つのパラグラフは3つの部分から構成されています。

Introduction	パラグラフが何について書かれているか？ 筆者があるトピックのどのような側面について、どのように考えているかを伝えます。
Discussion	Introductionで紹介したトピックや考えについて、説明や例、具体的な情報などを入れて、詳しく説明します（項目の数は決まっていませんが、この教科書では、主に3つの項目をあげて説明することを基本とします）。理由、原因、問題点、解決策、事例、証明、類似点と相違点などさまざまです。
Conclusion	結論文を書きます。Discussionのサマリーや筆者の考えをもう一度書いたり、まとめの言葉を添えます。ただし、1パラグラフの場合、まとめの言葉を書かない場合もあります。

実際に読んでみましょう。

「パラグラフって何？」の内容を英語にしたものです。これを読み、下の質問に答えましょう。

注意！　日本語の直訳ではありません。

English Paragraphs

Paragraphs are made up of three parts: an introduction, a discussion, and a conclusion. In the introduction, there is a topic sentence which includes a topic and a main idea. The topic is what the paragraph is about, and the main idea shows the writer's intention about the topic. In the discussion, there are usually three
5 supporting ideas with explanations, examples, and specific information. All of them must support the topic sentence. Depending on the type of topic sentence, however, these supporting ideas could be reasons, causes, problems, solutions, examples, evidence, similarities and differences, etc. In the conclusion, the topic sentence is stated again using different words, followed by a brief summary of the
10 supporting ideas, and a concluding sentence. Thus, the paragraph is a basic unit of written English that contains three parts.

Exercise 1: Introduction, discussion, conclusionの切れ目にスラッシュ（/）を入れましょう。

Exercise 2: Introductionとはなんですか？

Exercise 3: Discussionとはなんですか？

Exercise 4: Conclusionとはなんですか？

II　Content

なぜ私たちはGlobal relationsを学ばなければならないのでしょうか？　その重要性をここで確認します。指示に従い読んでみましょう。

A　Topic Introduction: **Learning about global relations**

Read the passage and answer the questions that follow. Share and check your answers with your team. Use the 'Language for Learning' expressions (see page 6).

1

International relations, international affairs, and global studies, are academic subjects in the fields of politics, economics, history, culture, society, and so on. They are all concerned with interactions among states, international organizations, and other actors in the global system. They also deal with shared issues like financial crisis, climate change, and human rights.

Question 1: Which of the following are not concerned with international relations, international affairs, and global studies?

a. The fields of politics, economics, history, culture, and society
b. Interactions in the global system and common global problems
c. Economic issues and public educational systems

> **Key terms**
>
> **concerned with** 〜関する　**interactions among** 〜間の交流　**actors** 国際主体（国家・国家共同体・多国籍企業など、国際的な行動力を行使できる組織体）　**global system** 国際システム（政治、経済、ビジネスなど）

2

In this textbook, you will learn about these kinds of global relations and issues. But why is such study important? Generally speaking, people usually care most about what is happening in their own country or community. But have you ever wondered how events in other countries affect you? Likewise, how are your decisions affecting people elsewhere? As you will learn, ideas, decisions, and activities in one part of the world are increasingly affecting societies far away. People are becoming more interconnected in almost every aspect of their lives: from the cultural and social to the economic and political.

Question 2: Studying about global relations and issues is important because _____.

a. people tend to care deeply about their country and community
b. things happening in one country are interconnected elsewhere
c. our choices affect cultural, social, economic, and political events

> **Key terms**
>
> **affect** 〜に影響を与える　**interconnected** 相互に関係のある、相互関連した

Let us consider an example. A politician's inappropriate comments about women can quickly <u>gain attention</u>, spreading globally, or '<u>going viral</u>', on social media. Consequently, widespread domestic and international <u>outcry</u> can force the politician to apologize and even lead to resignation. This brief example reflects
5 the spread of cultural values about gender equality. It also highlights the power of social media through which people are connecting and influencing events. In this case, probably for the public good.

Question 3: **Internet Search** ▶ For a social media post (video, Tweet, etc.) to be considered 'viral', how many views does it need? What are some recent examples of viral SNS posts in the field of global politics?

Key terms

gain attention 注目を集める　　going viral（インターネットやSNSで情報が）頻繁に共有される
outcry 抗議、非難

Through internet technologies we are able to <u>engage with</u> the world more than ever before. And our lives are becoming far more convenient. Yet, as societies and their peoples become more closely interconnected, misunderstanding, tension, and conflict can also arise. As such, it is important to understand the global
5 community from various perspectives and learn to express <u>informed opinions</u> about shared issues. We might then discover new ways to live more <u>harmoniously</u> and successfully with one another in this fast-changing world.

Question 4: What are advantages and disadvantages of a more closely connected world? How might we learn to live more peacefully and prosper?

Key terms

engage with ～と関わり合う　　informed opinions 情報に基づいた意見、見解　　harmoniously 調
和して

B Pair Discussion

The following discussion topics help you to think about your connections with the global community. In groups of four students, decide one or two questions you'd like to discuss. Use the 'Discussion Phrases' (see page 6).

1. How do ideas, decisions, or activities in Japan affect other countries?
2. Explain a recent international event, decision, or activity that has affected Japan.
3. Which foreign cultural values are influencing Japan? What is your opinion on that?
4. What connections do you have, or want to have, with the global community?
5. What is a specific example of tension or misunderstanding that can arise when two different cultures come into closer contact?

III Writing Task: Research and write about a piece of news you're interested in now.

興味のある国際関係に関するニュースについて120～130語程度で1パラグラフを書くことに挑戦してみましょう。
次のパラグラフはCOVID-19のワクチンにおける4か国の協力体制についてのパラグラフです。これを読み、質問に答えましょう。

A New Framework of Vaccines

Disc1-6
6))

    Japan, the US, Australia, and India created a framework for providing COVID-19 vaccines to developing countries, according to the Yomiuri Newspaper. After bigger, richer nations pushed past developing countries from Africa to the Andes for vaccines developed in the West, China began vaccine diplomacy
5 to expand its influence. In order to counter China's action, Japan and the other countries decided to provide low-interest loans so developing countries could buy vaccines made in India. In fact, Japan has helped these developing countries by sending funds through an international framework called COVAX. It was pointed out, however, that this action seemed to be anonymous because even though Japan
10 was helping people, no one would know where the money had come from.

(120 words)

Question 1　トピック・センテンスに波線を引きましょう。

Question 2　これは単なる慈善行為ではなく、1つの国の行為が他の国に影響を与えている例です。それが書かれているところを、（　　）で示しましょう。

Key terms

vaccines ワクチン　　diplomacy 外交　　expand 広げる　　counter 対抗する　　low-interest
loans 低金利ローン　　funds 資金　　anonymous 匿名

Bibliography

Chauvin, L. O., Failola, A., & Dou, E. (2021, March 10). Poorer nations turn to China in scramble for vaccine supply. *The Japan News*, 12.

Yomiuri Shimbun. (2021, March 10). Nichibeigouinn wakuchinn kyouyo. [Japan, the U.S., Australia, and India provided Vaccinations]. *Yomiuri Shimbun*, 1.

Your Writing

国際関係に関するニュースを120 〜 130語程度で1パラグラフ書いてみましょう。

Topic:

Topic sentence:

パラグラフの構成

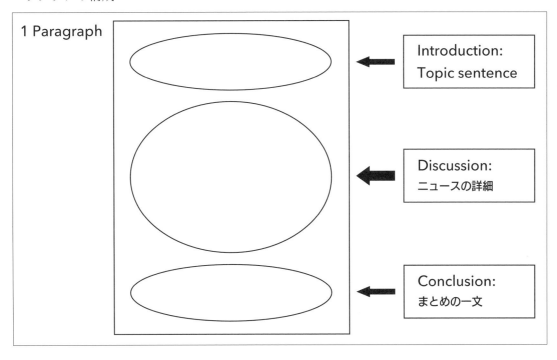

IV Grammar for Writing

A ニュースなど情報源を表すフレーズ

According to the Japan News,
According to Prof. Smith,
In the Daily Yomiuri,
Newsweek <u>says</u> that ～
（reports, explains, points out, states, indicates, argues, asserts, claims, maintains, etc.）

B 文って何?

文とは、2つ以上の語が集まり、主語と述語（動詞）から成りたっているものです。その1文だけで意味が成り立つものが主節、それだけでは成り立たないのが従属節です。because, as, as if, unless, although などの接続詞や that, what, which, who などの関係代名詞と使われ、主節との関係を表します。

主節と従属節の例：
Our lives have become more convenient because internet technologies are being developed.

Exercise 主節に下線を引きましょう。

1. International relations are related to social science, which is important too.
2. Since it is associated with diplomacy, it is difficult to solve.
3. The study of international relations began after WWI because establishing peace became very important.

Unit 2 The Big ideas in politics

Can Do
Structure: 英文の1パラグラフの構成を知る。
Content: いくつかのカギとなる政治的な要素についてある国を説明する。

S: Topic sentence や supporting sentences について学びます。
C: 国と国の問題を考える時、基本となる言葉や考え方があります。Sovereignty という考え方を取り上げて、1つの国を説明しましょう。

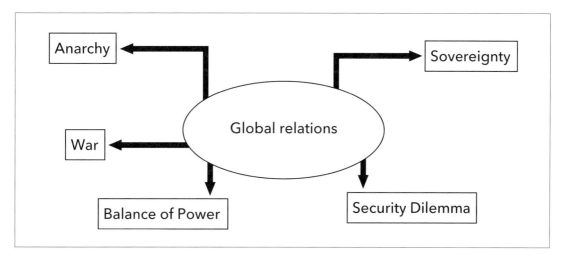

Anarchy

Sovereignty

War

Global relations

Balance of Power

Security Dilemma

I	Main idea topic sentences

パラグラフのメイン・アイディアを表現したものをトピック・センテンスと呼びます。多くの場合、パラグラフの最初のほうに置かれます。

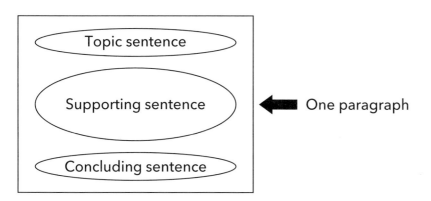

Topic sentence

Supporting sentence ◀— One paragraph

Concluding sentence

トピック・センテンスの前に導入文がはいることもあります。

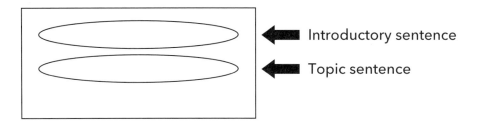

A) Topic sentenceとは

パラグラフの主題であるトピックについての筆者のメッセージのことを主題文（topic sentence）といいます。主題文では、明確に筆者の意見や伝えたいことを示さなければなりません。主題文は、パラグラフの最初に置きます（導入文が主題文の前にはいることもあります）。主題文はパラグラフで一番重要な文で、それ以外の文(supporting sentences＝支持文)は、この主題文に関係し、支持するものでなければなりません。トピック・センテンスは主題（topic）と主旨（controlling idea）と呼ばれる部分でできています。

トピックとは、「何について書かれているか」ということで、例えば日米関係について書かれているとします。しかし、「日米関係は双方にとって重要である」と書くのか、「日米関係は脆弱である」と書くのか、それぞれの筆者によって考えや書きたいことが違います。その筆者の考えを表しているのが、controlling idea と呼ばれるものです。つまり、パラグラフの内容を制御している、または、決めている考えということです。

Topic sentence = topic + controlling idea

B) 実際にTopic sentenceを読んでみましょう。

ポイント! 筆者の観点や意見が含まれているか、考えてみましょう。

Exercise 1: 次のトピック・センテンスを読んで、筆者の観点や意見が表れている部分に下線を引きましょう。

1. The issue of the Senkaku Islands presents a serious violation of sovereignty.
2. Japan should claim the Northern Territories.
3. The causes of global warming can be divided into four categories.
4. The balance of power is a basic strategy for countries to prevent war.
5. Terrorist attacks and civil wars are very different from each other.

Exercise 2: トピック・センテンスとして適切ではない理由を選びましょう。

1. About 500 million people were infected with the Spanish flu.　（　　）
2. The trade war between China and the US.　（　　）
3. Nuclear power is bad.　（　　）

> a. 主題文が大きすぎて、あいまいになっている。
> b. 事実だけを述べている。
> c. トピック（主題）だけを述べていて、筆者の考えがない

II Content

世界で今起こっていることを理解するには、いくつかの政治学上の概念を知っておくことは、大変役に立ちます。次の文章は、特に重要な3つの概念、sovereign state（主権国家）とbalance of power（力の均衡）とsecurity dilemma（安全保障のジレンマ）について紹介しています。

A Topic Introduction: **The big ideas in politics**

Read the passage and answer the questions that follow. Share and check your answers with your team. Use the 'Language for Learning' expressions (see page 6).

1

One of the most important political ideas is the sovereign state. A state is a political territory that is organized under one government. There are 206 sovereign states in the international political system. Sovereignty means that the government of a state has supreme, legal authority to make and enforce laws within its territory.
5 Sovereignty also means that a state is equal in the international political system. Other sovereign states in the international system must recognize and respect its authority. That is, states are not allowed to interfere in each other's domestic affairs. The United Nations, which is based on these principles, has 193 sovereign state members. In an era of rapid globalization, however, this concept of sovereignty has
10 become increasingly challenged.

Question 1: Who makes the law in a sovereign state?

Question 2: Upon what principles is the United Nations based?

Question 3: Internet Search ▶ Name three countries which are not members of the United Nations.

> **Key terms**
>
> **a sovereign state** 主権国家   **a political territory** 自治権をもつ領土・国土   the international
> **political system** 国際政治体制   **supreme, legal authority** 最高法的権威   **to interfere in** 〜に
> 干渉する

2

A second, important political idea is the balance of power. This concept describes a situation in which the power of a strong state or group of states (a coalition) is balanced by the power of other states. If a weak state is threatened

by a stronger state or coalition, it can make <u>allies</u> to protect itself and preserve its
5 own independence. Some academics argue that <u>state leaders</u> create and maintain a
balance of power through <u>international institutions and laws</u>. This is called a well-
planned or 'contrived' balance. Other academics claim that through alliances a
balance will <u>naturally emerge</u>, such as during <u>the Cold War</u> (1947 to 1991) between
the Soviet Union and the USA. This is referred to as an accidental or '<u>fortuitous</u>'
10 balance.

Question 4: Why do weak states make alliances with other states?

Question 5: What is the difference between the contrived and fortuitous balance of
power?

Question 6: Internet Search ▶ Name some of the countries which were allies with the Soviet
Union and the USA during the Cold War.

Key terms

balance of power 勢力均衡　　a coalition 連立　　to balance 均衡を保つ　　to threaten 威迫す
る、脅かす　　allies < an ally 同盟国、味方　　a state leader 国家元首、首脳　　international
institutions and laws 国際機関、国際法　　contrived 考案されたこと　　naturally emerge 自然に
出現する、自然に現れる　　the Cold War（東西の）冷戦　　fortuitous 自然に、偶然に

3

Disc1-9

A final idea that is useful to know is the *security dilemma*. According to some
academics, <u>the international political system</u> is considered to be 'anarchic'. This
means that there is no global government, or authority higher than <u>the state</u>, which
can <u>ensure order and security</u>. These academics argue that a state must ultimately
5 rely on itself to achieve security by increasing its own military power. Yet, when
one state increases its military power, foreign states might naturally question the
motives: Is it simply improving its <u>national defenses</u> or is it preparing to attack?
This uncertainty presents a dilemma to foreign states; that is, should they in turn
increase their own military power? Ironically, while states might be aiming to make
10 themselves more secure, the consequence is <u>a rising spiral of</u> insecurity.

Question 7: Why do some academics consider the international political system to be
anarchic?

Question 8: What is the security dilemma?

Question 9: Internet Search ▶ Find one or two contemporary examples of the security
dilemma.

B Team Quiz

Make teams of three. Take turns to ask each other a question in the order, 1 to 9.
Don't forget to use the 'Language for Learning' expressions (see page 6).

Quiz Questions

Student 1

Q1: The sovereign state has only one government. True or False?

Q4: If a weak state is threatened by a stronger state, it can make allies to protect itself
and its independence. True or False?

Q7: In the international political system, there is a global government, which is higher
than the sovereign state. True or False?

Student 2

Q2: There are 193 sovereign states in the international system. True or False?

Q5: State leaders can break a balance of power through international institutions and
laws. True or False?

Q8: A security dilemma can occur when states are uncertain about each other's military
motives. True or False?

Student 3

Q3: A sovereign state is equal in the international political system and other states must
not interfere in its domestic affairs. True or False?

Q6: When a balance of power happens naturally, it is called a 'fortuitous' balance. True
or False?

Q9: By increasing their military strength, states will increase their own security. True or
False?

III Writing Task: Research and write about one sovereign state.

3つの基本概念のうち、sovereigntyを考慮して、自分で選んだ国について1パラグラフを書きましょう。まず次の英文で構造を確認します。英文を読んで、質問に答えましょう。

The United Kingdom

The United Kingdom (UK) is a <u>multicultural</u> sovereign state with a leading role in world affairs. It is located in north-western Europe and is comprised of four nations: England, Wales, Scotland, and Northern Ireland. Its capital city is London, in England. The UK was <u>a founding member</u> of the United Nations (UN) 5 in 1945 and is one of the five permanent members of the UN Security Council, alongside China, France, Russia, and the USA. Its head of government is called the Prime Minister. The UK has a <u>multi-ethnic</u> population of about 67.8 million (UN data, 2020), of which approximately 87% are white, 3% black, 2.3% Indian, and 1.9% Pakistani (CIA World Factbook, 2021). From 1973, the UK became <u>a</u> 10 <u>prominent member state</u> of <u>the European Union (EU)</u>. However, in 2020, with the aim of regaining greater sovereignty, the UK left the EU. The British Exit, or <u>Brexit</u>, resulted in serious, ongoing political, economic, and social issues for the UK and EU. In short, the United Kingdom is a diverse country with an influential history, but its future is uncertain.

Question 1: Topic sentenceに波線を引きましょう。

Question 2: 現在の首相はだれか、どのような経歴かを調べましょう。

Question 3: どのような情報がいくつ書かれているのか、ペアで確認しましょう。

Key terms

multicultural 多文化的　a founding member 設立当初国　multi-ethnic 多民族の
a prominent member state 重要な加盟国　the European Union (EU) 欧州連合
Brexit ブレグジット（英国を表す形容詞 British と退出を意味する exit の混成語で、英国のEU離脱を指す用語）

References

CIA World Factbook. (2021). United Kingdom. In *World Factbook*. Retrieved March 6, 2021 from
　https://www.cia.gov/the-world-factbook/countries/

UN Data. (2020). United Kingdom. In *UN Data A world of information*. Retrieved March 6, 2021 from
　https://data.un.org/en/iso/gb.html

Your Writing

1つの sovereign state について、190 〜 210 words の1パラグラフを書きましょう。

Useful URLs: BBC Country Profiles
例：検索 bbc country profile united kingdom

World Bank
　・https://data.worldbank.org/country
UN (Sovereign) States
　・http://data.un.org/en/index.html
The World Factbook – CIA
　・https://www.cia.gov/the-world-factbook

Topic: ある1国
Topic sentence: その国を描写する代表的な一文

1パラグラフの構成

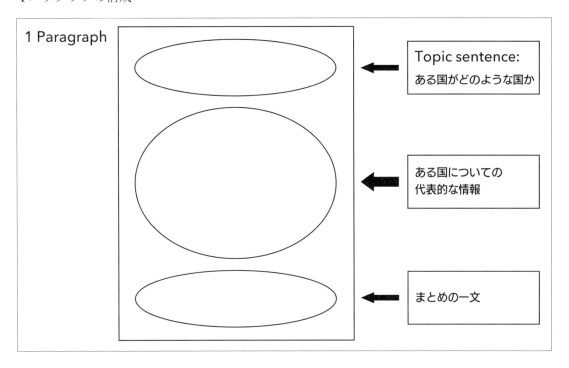

A) 位置（場所）を表すフレーズ

A is situated in the center of the country

A is located in a city

A is located on the north-east coast / an island

B)

2つの同等の独立した文を結びつける方法として for, and, nor, but, or, yet, so, などの等位接続詞でつなぐ方法があります。等位接続詞は7つしかないので、その頭文字をとって、FANBOYS と覚えておくと便利です。

Exercise　例文の意味を考えましょう。

for: It means *because*. It is usually used in more formal writing.

1. The research of war began after WWI, for people had become tired of conflict.

and: It means addition. It can also be used as *then* or *also*.

2. International relations is about political science and it is related to social science.

nor: It means a choice in negative phrases.

3. People did not understand why the war happened, nor did they understand how peace could be built.

but: It means *yet* or *on the contrary*.

4. Somalia is a sovereign state, but Somaliland is not internationally recognized as one.

or: It means lists of alternatives, or *otherwise*.

5. The UN has to stop the war or that small country will surely be destroyed completely.

yet: It means *though*, *still* or *nevertheless*.

6. Countries must protect their sovereign territory, yet they should try to avoid war at all costs.

so: It means *therefore*.

7. People wondered why the war happened, so they began to research about it.

Unit 3 — How do we see the world?

Can Do
Structure: 1つのパラグラフで、比較の構成について知る。
Content: さまざまな世界の政治形態を、2つ比べてみることで理解する。

S: 比較の構成と、coherence, cohesion そして unity を学びます。
C: International relations の中で、さまざまな政治や経済の形態を学びます。

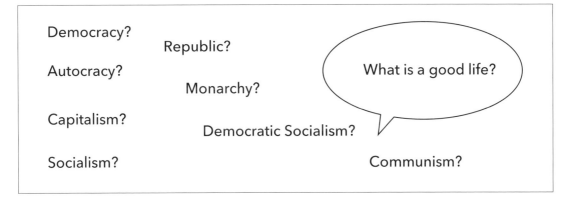

Democracy?
Republic?
Autocracy?
Monarchy?
Capitalism?
Democratic Socialism?
Socialism?
Communism?

What is a good life?

I Supporting sentences

A) Supporting sentences とは

1つのパラグラフには1つのトピック・センテンスがあります。そしてその主題文を説明する文が続きます。これを supporting sentences（支持文）と呼びます。この支持文は3つあることが多く、支持文1とその詳細、支持文2とその詳細、支持文3とその詳細のように書いていきます。これは、パラグラフの discussion の位置に書かれるもので、主題文を支持するものです。

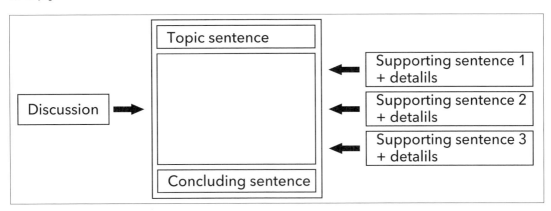

Topic sentence

Supporting sentence 1
+ detalils

Supporting sentence 2
+ detalils

Supporting sentence 3
+ detalils

Discussion

Concluding sentence

B）3つのライティングのポイント

よいライティングの条件は、unity（統一性）、coherence（一貫性）、cohesion（結束）が あるということです。

1. Unity（統一性）とは：

1つのパラグラフの中に、topic sentence（主題文）と関係ない文を入れないということです。この特性を統一性といいます。

2. Coherence（一貫性）とは：

1つのパラグラフの内容に一貫性があるということは、主題文で書かれた意見や考えに直接関連し、始めから終わりまで論理的に首尾一貫して書かれているということです。これには、3つのタイプがあります。

a. Narrative paragraphs and chronological ordering
   ある出来事などを時系列で述べる。

b. Descriptive paragraphs and spatial ordering
   言葉で絵を描く感覚で、空間的に、上から下に、左から右へ（その逆）、前から後ろ（その逆）などに描く。

c. Expository paragraphs and logical ordering
   論理や理由づけなどで、物事を論理的に説明する。

3. Cohesion（結束性）とは：

首尾一貫して書くために、1つのパラグラフの内容を論理的に関係づけていきます。この結びつきを結束性と呼びます。これは、大きく分けて3つの方法で行います。

a. 定冠詞を使う：a/an から the へ。
   複数形の名詞から the, those, these ＋複数名詞

b. 代名詞を使う：it, this, that, they, we, you, he, she, those, these, etc.

c. つなぎ言葉（transitions）で関係性を示す。例えば、furthermore, in addition, for example, first, second, however, in conclusion などがある（詳しくは Unit 5）。

次のパラグラフは、上の説明の内容を英語にしたものです（ただし、一字一句訳したものではありません）。これを読み、下の質問に答えましょう。

....

Characteristics of a good paragraph: unity, coherence, and cohesion Disc1-11 11))

In English, a well-written paragraph has unity, coherence, and cohesion. What does this mean? First, all the supporting sentences should relate to the topic sentence. This characteristic is called unity and means to exclude any sentences irrelevant to the topic sentence. Next is coherence. A paragraph has coherence

5 when the supporting sentences are ordered and explained logically. There are three types of ordering; chronological ordering, spatial ordering, and logical ordering.

Each one has a long history. The last characteristic is cohesion. This means all the supporting sentences are connected by pronouns, definite articles, and connectors called transitions. Thus, these are the three well-defined characteristics for writing
10 a good paragraph.

Exercise 1: スラッシュ（/）を入れて３つの部分に分けましょう。

Exercise 2: ３つのsupporting sentencesの始まりの単語を四角で囲みましょう。

Exercise 3: トピック・センテンスとは関係ない文が一文入っています。どれですか？　消去すべき文に打ち消し線を引きましょう。

Exercise 4: このパラグラフのcoherenceは、３つのorderingのうちどれですか？

Exercise 5: Cohesionは、冠詞、代名詞、つなぎ言葉で文を関係づけていきますが、それぞれ下線を引いて示しましょう。

II　Content

世界を理解するために、２つの重要な政治理論を紹介します。２つの考え方を説明し、その違いを理解します。指示に従い読んでみましょう。

A　Topic Introduction: **How do we see the world?**

Read the passage and highlight these verbs: **accept, argue, assert, claim, maintain, and recognize**. These verbs introduce a point of view. (See also Unit 8, Grammar for Writing.)

Disc1-12

For centuries, rulers, governments, and their people have tried to make sense of the world around them. While there are numerous theories to explain global interactions, it is helpful to start with two main political schools of thought, namely liberalism and realism. These two theories have some similarities, yet they
5 both remain different in their core principles.

How Liberalism Sees the World

There are many varieties of liberalism but the main principle is that the human race can improve and democracies are necessary for this to happen. Liberalism maintains that peace and security in international society comes from
10 the many international laws, procedures, rules, and norms. Although liberalism accepts that the state is an important actor in global interactions, it does not

accept that the state is the main actor. Instead, liberalism argues that there are numerous other influential actors, such as <u>multinational corporations</u> (e.g., Apple), <u>transnational groups</u> (e.g., INGOs such as Human Rights Watch), and

15 intergovernmental organizations (e.g., <u>IGOs</u> such as the United Nations). Because states have to cooperate with each other and many other actors, they cannot behave with complete freedom. As such, liberalism asserts that <u>interdependence</u> between states and other actors is a critically important feature of how the world works. Creating an international society where all states gain through cooperation

20 is crucial to improving everyone's <u>well-being</u>.

Key terms

schools of thought ～学派   liberalism 自由主義   realism 写実主義、現実主義
core principles ～の中核原理   democracies 民主主義   international laws, procedures, rules, and norms 国際法、国際手続き、国際規定、国際規範   actor アクター、主体
multinational corporations 多国籍企業   transnational groups 国境を超えるグループ・組織
INGOs (International Non-Governmental Organizations) 国際非政府組織   well-being 福祉
IGOs (intergovernmental organizations) 国際組織   interdependence 相互依存

How Realism Sees the World

Realism, as the name suggests, claims to offer a more 'realist' explanation of how the world works. In contrast to liberalism, it can be said that realism has a far more <u>pessimistic worldview</u>. A core principle of realism is that human beings are <u>ultimately self-centred</u>, and so the significant improvement of global interactions

5 is <u>highly improbable</u>. Realism maintains that peace and security in international society comes from a <u>balance of power</u>, in which each state tries <u>to prevent</u> others <u>from dominating</u>. As such, there is always the threat of war and so <u>maintaining a military advantage</u> is crucial. Realism recognizes the role of various actors in global society such as the United Nations and <u>NGOs</u>. However, it argues that

10 because all other actors must work under <u>the sovereign state system</u>, there is <u>no higher authority than</u> the sovereign state. While realism recognizes that states can achieve their goals through <u>bargaining</u>, <u>alliances</u>, and cooperation, it asserts that when states cooperate, they will always try to gain more than their rivals.

Key terms

a pessimistic worldview 厭世観   ultimately self-centred 結局自己中心的、身勝手の極み
highly improbable ほとんどありそうもない   balance of power 勢力均衡   to prevent from dominating ～を支配しないようにする   to maintain a military advantage 軍事的優位を保つ
NGOs (Non-Governmental Organizations) 非政府組織   the sovereign state system 主権国家体制   no higher authority than ～ ～より高い権威がない   bargaining 交渉   alliances 同盟

B) Political Points of View

1. Cover the reading passage! In groups of three or four students, share out the 'point-of view' sentences (A to L) below.

    A. Humans can improve and democracy is necessary for this to happen.
    B. When a state cooperates, it should always try to gain more than its rival.
    C. States do not have complete freedom to behave as they like.
    D. Not only states, but other actors are also influential in global interactions.
    E. Cooperation is important for achieving a state's goals.
    F. Order in the world is based on international laws, norms, and so on.
    G. Humans are selfish, so improving the human race is unlikely.
    H. Because war is a constant threat, a strong military is crucial.
    I. In global society, there is no higher authority than the sovereign state.
    J. International society works best when all states gain through cooperation.
    K. States are an important actor in global interactions.
    L. Order in the world is based on the balance of power.

2. Match the 'point-of view' sentences (A to L) to either liberalism, realism, or both theories (in the middle). Write the letter on the Venn diagram below. If you are not sure of the answer, look again at the reading passage.

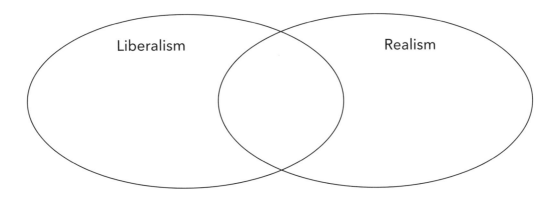

Liberalism   Realism

III   **Writing Task: Research and write about types of government.**

人類は、どのような政治・経済の形が私たちによりよい生活をもたらすのかと長い間追及してきました。その結果、さまざまな政治・経済の形を作り試してきました。このユニットの冒頭にもありますが、代表的なものは次のようなものです。democracy, autocracy, capitalism, socialism, communism
そして、最近では、democratic socialism という形態もでてきました。これらを知ることは、

さまざまな国の歴史、また他の国との関係の歴史、そして現在の状況を理解することに役に立ちます。

これらを理解するために、2つの形の政治・経済の在り方を比べながら、重要な特徴を説明するというライティングを行います。次のサンプルは、民主主義と独裁政治を比べたものです。これを読み、質問に答えましょう。

Democracy vs. Autocracy

　　　Many western countries and Japan have enjoyed a long history of democracy for their <u>citizens</u>. However, it is also true that some countries have experienced autocracy. Because of this, we can see that there are some advantages and disadvantages regarding these two very different types of government. Firstly, in
5　a democracy, all citizens have power and <u>an equal say</u> about their lives. However, in an autocracy, one leader has the power to make decisions about people's lives. Secondly, in a democracy, citizens have not only freedom of thought and opinion, but also freedom of expression. This creates a system of checks and balances on the government. In an autocracy, however, one leader, called <u>a dictator</u> or <u>autocrat</u>,
10　prohibits people from expressing their opinion, and can even punish them if they disagree with the leader's ideas. Thirdly, in a democracy, since everyone can express their opinion freely, it often takes a long time to make decisions. However, in an autocracy, decisions can be made quickly because only the leader has to decide. Lastly, a democracy seems more likely to come up with good ideas for everyone
15　because many people are involved. Yet this does not mean the country is always led by good decisions. For example, if the majority of citizens have bad ideas, the country will move in the wrong direction. But in an autocracy, if the leader is smart, the country will be led by good decisions. If not, the opposite will happen without anyone able to stop them. Thus, even though we know which form of government
20　seems better for people, both democracy and autocracy have advantages and disadvantages.

> **Key terms**
>
> autocracy 専制政治（独裁政治）　citizens 市民　　an equal say 平等な発言権　　a dictator 独裁者
> an autocrat 独裁君主

Question 1: スラッシュ（/）を入れて3つの部分に分けましょう。

Question 2: 4つのsupporting sentencesの最初の単語を四角で囲みましょう。

Question 3: 文と文の間のtransitions（つなぎ言葉）に波線を引きましょう。

Question 4: 次のアウトラインの空欄を埋めましょう。

Topic: Democracy and Autocracy
Topic sentence: There are several advantages and disadvantages of a democracy and an autocracy.

Advantages and disadvantages of a democracy and an autocracy

A. The power to make decisions about citizens' lives

    1. In a democracy, the _____ have power.

    2. In an autocracy, one _____ has power.

B. Freedom

    1. In a democracy, the citizens have freedom of _____ and opinion, and freedom of _____ .

    2. In an autocracy, the citizens don't have freedom. The leader prevents others from expressing their opinions and can even _____ them if they _____ with the leader's ideas.

C. Making decisions

    1. In a democracy, it takes _____ to make decisions because everyone can express their opinion freely.

    2. In an autocracy, decisions can be made _____ because only the _____ has to decide.

D. Possibility of having good ideas

    1. A democracy is more likely to have good ideas because _____ are involved, but this _____ that the country will always be led by good decisions.

    2. In an autocracy, if the leader is _____ , it is possible to have a good idea, but if not, _____ will happen without anyone able to stop it.

Your Writing

自分で興味のあるトピックを決めて、1パラグラフ書きましょう

Examples of your topic sentences:
There are several advantages and disadvantages of capitalism and socialism.
There are more advantages than disadvantages to adopting democratic socialism.

China has taken a new course of using capitalism in a communist country.

Topic:
Topic sentence:

パラグラフの構成

> Topic sentence
> Different point 1
> Different point 2
> Different point 3
> Concluding sentence

Ⅳ Grammar for Writing

A) 基本のつなぎ言葉
例：for example, for instance
順：first (firstly), second (secondly), third (thirdly), finally
反対の事柄：however, but, yet
結論：in conclusion, in summary, thus

B) such as の使い方
such as ＋名詞（具体例）
○ Countries such as the US, Japan, and France are democracies.
　Countries と such as の間にカンマがないということは、必要な情報であるということです。
× Countries, such as the US, Japan, and France, are democracies.
　カンマを付けると、付け足しの意味になり、Countries are democracies. となっても意味が通ることが必要です。
　ここでは、どの国も民主主義という意味になって、独裁主義、専制的な国も存在するので、「まちがった文」になってしまいます。

C) 前置詞を含む連語（Democracy vs. Autocracy から）
because of ～ ,　　　　　prohibit from ～ ,
disagree with ～ ,　　　 come up with ～ ,
in the direction,

Exercise （→ p. 120 参照）

Unit 4
The development of international society

Can Do

Structure: Coherenceの１つである、chronological orderingで書く。
Content: 政治的に重要な出来事を書けるようにする。

S: 起こった年月を順を追って書くことを学びます。
C: International relations の中でも特に政治的に重要な出来事を学びます。

I Coherence: narrative, descriptive, and expository writing

　　Unit 3で学習したgood writingの3つの要素のうちの1つ、cohesionにはそのトピックとその書く文章の目的によって、3つのアプローチがあります。

1) Narrative paragraphs and chronological ordering (time order)
　　ある出来事などを時系列で述べる。
2) Descriptive paragraphs and spatial ordering
　　言葉で絵を描く感覚で、空間的に、上から下に、左から右へ（その逆）、前から後ろ（その逆）などに描く。
3) Expository paragraphs and logical ordering
　　これは、論理や理由づけなどで、物事を論理的に説明する。

実際に読んでみましょう。

Coherenceの内容を英語にしたものです。これを読み、下の質問に答えなさい。

注意！　日本語の直訳ではありません。

Coherence

One of the most important characteristics for good writing is coherence. To achieve this there are three types of paragraphs and ordering. One type is narrative paragraphs with chronological ordering. Narrative paragraphs include stories and biographies. Therefore, the supporting sentences are usually ordered according
5　to when the events happened. However, some recent works mix the past and the present. The second one is descriptive paragraphs with spatial ordering. These describe objects such as people, rooms, locations, and events according to how our eyes see things. For example, they can be described from top to bottom, right to left, front to back, and vice versa. The third one is expository paragraphs with
10　logical ordering. Expository paragraphs have a full explanation based on logic and reason that reflects a writer's point of view. In short, coherence provides supporting sentences with one of three types of ordering that makes them easy to understand.

Exercise 1:　スラッシュ（/）を入れて３つの部分（introduction, discussion and conclusion）に分けましょう。

Exercise 2:　トピック・センテンスに下線を引きましょう。

Exercise 3:　３つのsupporting sentencesの始まりのフレーズを四角で囲みましょう。

Exercise 4:　Cohesionのための冠詞、代名詞、つなぎ言葉を（　　）に入れましょう

Exercise 5:　トピック・センテンスとは関係ない文が一文入っています。どれですか？　消去すべき文に打ち消し線を引きましょう。

▌II　Content

国際関係において、平和の構築へのプロセスには、重要な出来事がいくつかあります。その内容についてここで確認します。指示に従い読んでみましょう。

Ⓐ　Topic Introduction: **The development of international society**

Read the passage and answer the questions that follow. Share and check your answers with your team. Use the 'Language for Learning' expressions (see page 6).

1

The Peace of Westphalia (1648) was a key event in the development of the contemporary international political system. **In 1648**, the Holy Roman Empire, the major power in Europe, gave sovereign equality to a significant number of its states, which meant non-intervention in their domestic affairs. (**Before 1648**, states were under the Holy Roman Empire's supreme authority.) **After 1648**, hundreds of mini-states still existed, but the interaction between ten key states began to determine events in international society.

Question 1: What did the Holy Roman Empire agree to do? Why do you think that was important?

Question 2: How did international society change after this event?

> ─ **Key terms** ─
>
> **The Peace of Westphalia** ヴェストファーレン条約（ウェストファリア条約）　**the Holy Roman Empire** 神聖ローマ帝国　**sovereign equality** 主権平等　**non-intervention in domestic affairs** 内政不干渉　**under ~ authority** ~の支配［権力］下に　**supreme authority** 最高権威

2

From 1815, the leading states in Europe established the Concert of Europe. This coalition of powerful states aimed to make collective decisions on various contentious issues while maintaining a permanent European 'balance of power.' In 1815, the coalition redrew the map of Europe to implement this plan. However, during the 19th century, nationalism, militarism, rival alliances, and competition for resources developed across Europe. The outcome was World War I (1914~18), which brought about an end to the Concert of Europe.

Question 3: What two aims did the Concert of Europe want to achieve?

Question 4: What were the reasons for the end of the Concert of Europe?

Question 5: [Internet Search ▶] What were the five member states of the Concert of Europe?

> ─ **Key terms** ─
>
> **leading states** 強国　**the Concert of Europe** ヨーロッパ協調　**coalition** 連立、連合　**aim to** ねらう、目指す　**collective decisions** 共同（的意思）決定　**permanent** 永続的な　**redrew the map of Europe** ヨーロッパの地図を塗り替える・国境線を引き直す　**implement** 実行する　**nationalism** 民族主義、国粋主義　**militarism** 軍国主義　**rival alliances** 国家間（の）［各国間の］競争　**bring about an end to** ~に終わり［終結］をもたらす、~を終わらせる

3

After the First World War, the League of Nations was established in 1920. Unlike the former Concert of Europe, membership was worldwide, and by 1935 the League of Nations had 58 member states (the United States refused to join). In the 1930s, Germany, Italy, Japan, and Russia, all had governments with extremist ideologies and wanted to expand their territories, and from 1939 to 1945 the world was once again at war.

Question 6: How was the Concert of Europe and the League of Nations different?

Question 7: How many member states were there in 1935?

Question 8: What were the reasons for the end of the League of Nations?

Key terms

the League of Nations 国際連盟（国家間の協力と平和を促進させるために1920年に形成された国際機関）
former 元の、以前の　**the Concert of Europe** ヨーロッパ協調　**extremist ideologies** 過激派の
（過激な）思想［考え方・イデオロギー］　**expand territories** 領土を拡張する

4

When the Second World War ended in 1945, a stronger version of the League of Nations was established. This organization was called the United Nations (UN), which initially had 51 members. However, the Cold War (1947~1991) between the United States and the Soviet Union (the two most important members of the UN Security Council) divided the world into two competing international societies. With the end of the Cold War in 1991, the United States became the global superpower, and a new era of international society began based on Western principles of liberal democracy.

Question 9: What was established in 1945; and how many members did it have?

Question 10: Why was international society still divided after 1945?

Question 11: On what principles was society based after 1991; and why?

Key terms

the United Nations (UN) 国際連合　**the Cold War** 冷戦　**the UN Security Council** 国連安全
保障理事会　**global superpower** 地球規模の超大国　**Western principles of liberal democracy**
西洋自由民主主義の原理

The three phrases in bold in Paragraph 1 describe when something happened. Try to find 12 more expressions in Paragraph 2, 3, and 4. What other expressions can we use to describe time order? Write them in the box.

Time Order Expressions in the Passage:		
1.	5.	9.
2.	6.	10.
3.	7.	11.
4.	8.	12.

Other Time Order Expressions:

C) **History Timeline**

Summarize the development of international history. Use the time-order expressions that you studied above.

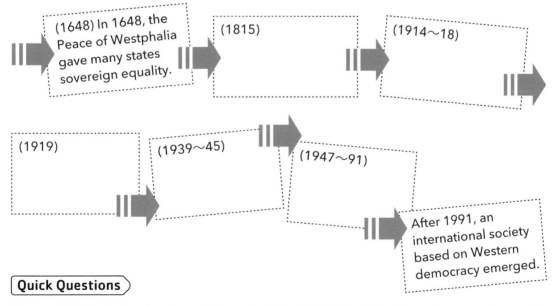

Quick Questions

The world didn't stop turning at the end of the Cold War. What have been major events in the development of international society since 1991? Why do you think they are important? Discuss with a partner, then write your sentences (your idea + supporting reason). Be sure to use the 'Language for Learning' and 'Discussion Phrases' (see page 6).

Writing Task: Research and write about historical incidents.

歴史上の重要な出来事について調べて書いてみましょう。次のパラグラフはキューバ危機についてのパラグラフです。これを読み、質問に答えましょう。

Cuban Missile Crisis

Disc1-20
20)))

Even since World Wars I and II, we have experienced dangerous moments that could have led to World War III. One of them was the Cuban Missile Crisis which happened during the Cold War. On October 14, 1962, an American U-2 spy plane discovered a Soviet <u>ballistic missile</u> being assembled in Cuba. The US and
5　Cuba had a <u>hostile</u> relationship after Fidel Castro <u>overthrew</u> Batista's government that was supported by the US. The US responded by <u>imposing economic sanctions,</u> and later launched <u>a failed attack</u> on Cuba. Because of this, Cuba approached the Soviet Union. The Soviets also felt <u>insecure</u> about the US having nuclear weapons in Europe and Turkey. On October 22, after an <u>intense</u> discussion with <u>the Executive</u>
10　<u>Committee of the National Security Council</u>, President Kennedy announced that the US would establish <u>a blockade</u> around Cuba instead of directly attacking the country. On October 24, the sea around Cuba was blocked by the US to prevent the Soviets from <u>delivering</u> missiles to Cuba. The Soviet Union could have attacked the US in response to this act. However, instead, on October 26, Khrushchev sent
15　a message to Kennedy in which he proposed <u>removing</u> the missiles in exchange for the US not attacking Cuba. On October 27, although a US plane was shot down over Cuba, Kennedy agreed not to attack. As a result, on October 28, Khrushchev agreed to remove Soviet missiles from Cuba. In conclusion, the Cuban Missile Crisis was a stressful thirteen days for the entire world.

Question 1: トピック・センテンスに波線を引きましょう。

Question 2: スラッシュ（/）を入れて、このパラグラフを3つの部分 introduction, discussion and conclusion)に分けましょう。

Question 3: 6つのsupporting sentencesの始まりのフレーズを四角で囲みましょう（通常3つのことが多いのですが、出来事がたくさんある場合はそれ以上のことがあります）。

Question 4: Time orderの単語やフレーズに（　）を付けましょう。

Question 5: アウトラインの空欄を埋めましょう。（→p. 121 参照）

Key terms

ballistic missile 弾道弾ミサイル　　hostile 敵対的な　　overthrow 打倒する
impose economic sanctions 経済制裁を課す　　a failed attack 失敗した攻撃　　insecure 不安な
intense 激しい　　the Executive Committee of the National Security Council 国家安全保障会
議の執行委員会　　a blockade 封鎖　　deliver 届ける　　removing 取り除く

Writing Task

国際政治の歴史の中で、自分の興味あるトピックを選び、coherence の中の chronological ordering を意識して、1パラグラフ書いてみましょう。

Examples of your topics:
WWI, WWII, the Korean War, other civil wars, other war-related events

Examples of your topic sentences:
1. World War I started with several major causes.
2. The Korean War started with complicated reasons.
3. The Chechen conflict with the Russian government had a long history.

Ⅳ　Grammar for Writing

A. Chronological ordering の英文書くためには、時を表す表現が必要です。

1. Expressions of Time

a. at, on, in

at: ちょうどを表す

I get up at 7 o'clock.　My school starts at 8: 30.　We arrived at 10:45.
(at lunchtime　　at sunset　　at night)

on: 曜日や日付

I will see you on Monday.　　　We will leave on June 15.
(on her birthday　　on Christmas Day　　on weekends)

in: 月・年・季節

The first semester starts in April.　　My son was born in 2020.
We can see many flowers in spring.
(in the 18th century　　in the past　　in the future)

b. 注意すべき使い方

in ＋期間は「〜後に」という意味になる。

I'll see you at the entrance in 5 minutes. (5分後に会う)
They'll leave for the US in 6 months.　(6か月後にアメリカに行く。)

in the morning　　in the afternoon　　in the evening

限定されると on

on Friday morning(s)　　on Monday afternoon(s)
on the evening of August 8, 2021

next, last, this, that がつくと、前置詞が省略される。

We'll see you next Wednesday.　　They went to a concert last Friday.
I'll come home this Saturday.

c. one, any, each, every, some, all がつくと、前置詞が省略される。

You can come to see me anytime.　　　They greet each other every morning.

d. until と by

until:「～まで」という動作・状態の継続を表す。by:「～までに」という期限を表す。

I have to finish my report by Monday morning.

I will work on my report until Monday morning. (Then, I can go shopping.)

f. for, while, during

for は期間を表すので、for のあとには数詞が来ることが多い。

while は「～の間」という意味を表すが、while のあとは、S + V（節）が来る。

during:「～の間」という意味を表すが、during のあとは名詞が来る。

We've been studying English for more than 6 years.

Her mother was in a coffee shop while her daughter was taking a class.

It rained heavily during the night.

Exercise 1:　at, on, in のうちいずれかを入れましょう（どれも必要がないときは、×）。

1. She came to my house (　　　　　　　) Tuesday.
2. I'll be coming (　　　　　　) ten minutes.
3. I don't take a walk (　　　　　　　) night.
4. My son was born (　　　　　　) the morning of June 3, 2020.
5. That fashion became popular (　　　　　　) the 1990s.
6. What do you do (　　　　　　) Christmas?
7. They took a trip to the UK (　　　　　　　) last January.
8. We like to watch movies (　　　　　　) weekends.

Exercise 2:　by, until, for, during, while のいずれかを入れましょう。

1. Students have to hand in this report (　　　　　　　) Thursday.
2. I stayed in Japan (　　　　　　) the end of July.
3. We lived in the US (　　　　　　) 4 years.
4. He fell asleep (　　　　　　) the movie.
5. The man continued to cough (　　　　　　　) he was on the train.
6. We had a lot of accidents (　　　　　　) the trip.
7. My mother will get angry if I don't come home (　　　　　　　) 10 o'clock.
8. I'll be working (　　　　　　) 5 o'clock. So, I'll see you at 5:30.

B. Spatial ordering の英文書くためには、場所・位置を表す表現が必要です。

1. Expressions of locations

next to	between	close to	behind
above	below	in front of	in the front of
in back of	in the back of	in the middle of	in the center of
to the right of	to the left of	on the right	on the left
at the edge of	in the north of	in the south of	in the east of
in the west of	on the opposite side of		

Exercise 3:（→ p. 122 参照）

Unit 5 Globalization

Can Do
Structure: エッセイの構成を知る。
Content: Globalizationのメリットとデメリットについて考える。

S: エッセイの構成を学び、書けるようにします。
C: Globalizationとは実際どういうことなのかを学習し、そのメリットとデメリットを考えます。

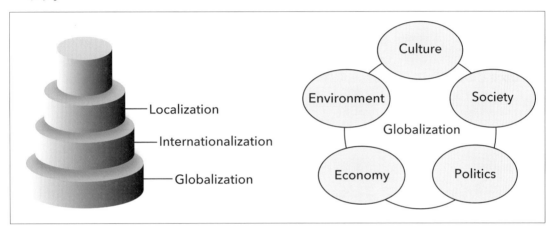

Essay Writing

ここでいうエッセイは、「小論」や「論説」を意味します。筆者の感想や見聞をまとめた「随筆」とは異なります。また、エッセイはいくつかのパラグラフで成り立っています。本論のところが1パラグラフ、2パラグラフ、3パラグラフ、4パラグラフ、5パラグラフ、それ以上といろいろあります。

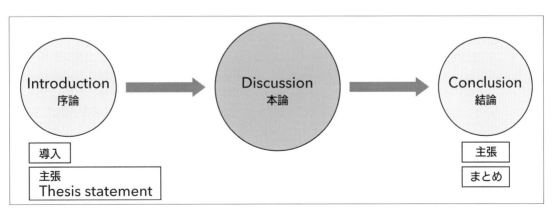

A) Essayとは？

　Essayとは、学術的な文章の書き方（academic writing）で書かれた、論文やレポートのことを指します。ある考えや主張を、リサーチをし、根拠になる事実や証拠を示しながら、論理的に説明し、読み手を説得します。

　エッセイは、複数のパラグラフから成り（ここでは5パラグラフ書きますが、その数は決まっているわけではありません）、1パラグラフの時と同じく、introduction, discussion (body), conclusionという3つの部分で構成されています。1つのパラグラフの場合、最初にtopic sentenceを置きますが、それがエッセイでは、thesis statementと呼ばれ、第1パラグラフの最後に置きます。これは、エッセイ全体の主張または議論をまとめた文章のことです。次のdiscussionの部分は、支持パラグラフ（supporting paragraphs）とも呼ばれ、出だしは、それぞれのパラグラフのメインになる考えをまとめたtopic sentenceで始めます。そして最後に、結論の1パラグラフを書きます。ここには、thesis statementを別の言葉で言い直したものと、discussionで書いた理由、問題、原因などをもう1度繰り返すか、それをまとめた文を書き、その後に結論文を書きます。

B) エッセイの構成

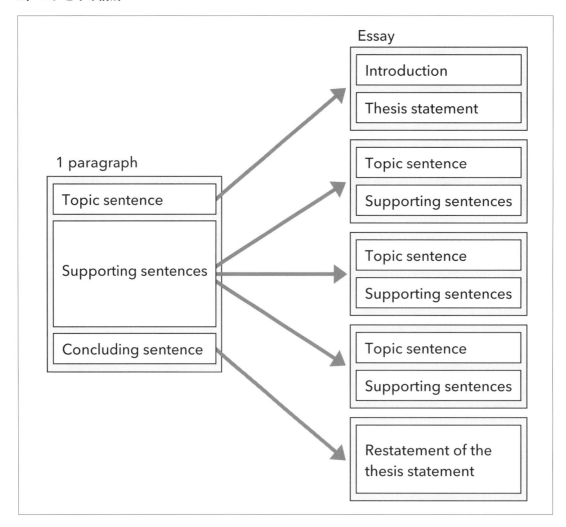

II Content

私たちはグローバリゼーションという言葉をよく耳にします。しかし、それは実際どういう意味なのでしょうか？　まず自分で考え、その後クラスで話しあってみてください。

A Topic Introduction: **Globalization**

Read the passage and answer the questions that follow. Share and check your answers with your team. Use the 'Language for Learning' expressions (see page 6).

Globalization is a process of growing <u>interconnectedness</u> between societies. It is not a recent phenomenon; however, three <u>characteristics</u> distinguish contemporary globalization from that of earlier periods in history.

The first characteristic of <u>contemporary</u> globalization is the scale of its
5 extensity. This means that events in one part of the world have an increasing effect on societies far away. One example is the conflicts in Syria, Afghanistan, and Iraq, which resulted in <u>unprecedented numbers</u> of people fleeing their countries between 2014 and 2019. The <u>subsequent</u> arrival of these migrants in the European Union led to serious ongoing <u>social and political upheaval</u> across the region.

Question 1: What is the extensity characteristic of globalization?

Another characteristic of contemporary globalization is its growing intensity. This means that <u>aspects of one society</u> are becoming more deeply interconnected with those of another. These aspects are political, economic, cultural, social (e.g., information, educational systems, and migration), military, ecological, legal,
5 and technological. However, some aspects are more deeply interconnected than others. For instance, we can say that economic globalization is far more intensive than cultural globalization.

Question 2: What is the intensity characteristic of globalization?
Question 3: Which aspects of society are affected?

A further characteristic of contemporary globalization is its velocity.

Sophisticated transportation and <u>technological innovations</u> have increased the speed with which people, ideas, information, goods, and <u>capital</u> are moving around the world. This has obvious benefits, but also drawbacks. Think about the rapid

5 spread of the Covid-19 pandemic and <u>global financial crisis</u> which resulted.

In spite of such controversies, contemporary globalization appears resilient and marks a new era <u>in the evolution of</u> international society.

- -

Question 4: What is the velocity characteristic of globalization?

Key terms

interconnectedness 相互関連性   a characteristic of 〜の特徴   contemporary 現在の
unprecedented numbers 前例のないほど多くの〜   subsequent 続く   social and political
upheaval 社会的・政治的激変   aspect of society 社会の側面   technological innovations 技
術革新   capital 資本、資金   global financial crisis 世界金融危機   in the evolution of 〜の進
歩の点で

(B) **Team Quiz**

Make teams of three. Take turns to ask each other a question in the order, 1 to 9.
Don't forget to use the 'Language for Learning' (see page 6).

(**Quiz Questions**)

Student 1

Q1: Globalization is a process of growing interconnectedness between societies. True or False?

Q4: Intensity means that almost every aspect of our society is becoming interconnected with other societies. True or False?

Q7: The velocity characteristic of globalization means the speed with which people, ideas, information, goods, and capital are moving around the world. True or False?

Student 2

Q2: Four characteristics distinguish contemporary globalization from that of earlier periods in history. True or False?

Q5: There are at least six aspects of society which are becoming global. True or False?

Q8: The velocity of globalization can be good and bad. True or False?

Student 3

Q3: Extensity means that events in one part of the world happen very quickly. True or False?

Q6: Some aspects of society are more globalized than others. True or False?

Q9: Globalization is likely to develop further in the future. True or False?

C Think, Pair-Share: **Recognizing the Effects of Globalization**

Match political, economic and social globalization [P], [E], and [S] with their effects (1) to (9). Then, write a sentence and share your answers with a partner.

Table 1

	Political [P]	Economic [E]	Social [S]
P, E	(1) more companies outsourcing abroad	(4) increased foreign tourism	(7) unemployment in some industries
	(2) challenges to local custom and culture	(5) improvements in human rights	(8) social movements like #me too
	(3) international agreements on climate change	(6) organizations like the United Nations	(9) more trade between distant countries

Example Sentence: "I think political and economic globalization **leads to** more companies outsourcing abroad. How about you?"

Other useful verbs:
brings about, causes, results in

D **Three-Step Discussion**

First, prepare your ideas about the topic in Japanese. Share and develop your ideas with your home team and then write out an opinion in English. Make new groups and share/discuss your ideas in English. Be sure to use your 'Language for Learning' and 'Discussion Phrases' (see page 6).

Discussion Question: In your view, do the effects (1) to (9) in Table 1 represent advantages or disadvantages of globalization; are they positive or negative? Could some effects represent both?

Example response: "Political globalization leads to more companies outsourcing abroad. In my opinion, this is an advantage because Japanese companies can produce products at a lower cost overseas. On the other hand, it can be a disadvantage to local workers who might receive low wages and work in poor conditions."

III **Writing Task:** Identify advantages and/or disadvantages of specific aspects of globalization.

ここでは、globalizationのメリットもしくはデメリットについて書くことが課題ですが、その前に例文で構造を確認します。次のエッセイはglobalizationに関係の深いlocalizationについてのエッセイです。これを読み、質問に答えましょう。

Localization

It is impossible to understand world issues without first considering the various aspects of globalization. In terms of economic globalization, to be successful in business, people need to use the strategy of localization. Localization means that some products and services are changed to suit local taste and needs.
5 There are three major reasons why this strategy is important.

The first reason is that entry into foreign markets becomes much easier. When companies try to expand beyond their own country, they face a lot of difficulties, such as laws about distribution, cultural differences, and communication. When their products and services can be adapted to specific targets and local markets,
10 they appeal to local people. By offering unique products and services, companies can avoid some of the difficulties in culture and communication.

The second reason is that localization will satisfy more customers and increase overall sales figures eventually. In the case of TOYOTA, if they know that local people need four-wheel drive cars rather than ordinary passenger cars because
15 of where they live, the company can focus on selling these. As a result, customer satisfaction will increase and other types of cars might also be sold because the company can gain trust in the local market.

Last, but certainly not least, is that by increasing sales a company gains power to compete locally as well as internationally. This helps a company to grow globally, which is the essence of globalization. In the age we are living in, a mega-number of
20 goods and services are available to a global market. And so, a company can expect an enormous amount of profit and establish a widely known brand name.

As you can see, localization is an important part of globalization. It enables easy access to foreign markets, localized products and services increase customer
25 satisfaction, and it leads to higher sales figures. Thus, a company gains power locally and internationally, and achieves globalization.

Question 1: Thesis statement に波線を引きましょう。

Question 2: 3つの理由に二重線を引き、簡単に日本語で説明しましょう。

Key terms

strategy 作戦、戦略　　distribution 流通　　adapted 適合させる　　sales figures 売り上げの数字
four-wheel drive cars 四輪駆動　　enable できるようにする

References

Lionbridge. (2020, January 4). *Localization, globalization, internationalization: What's the difference?* Retrieved March 23, 20222 from https://www.lionbridge.com/blog/translation-localization/localization-globalization-internationalization-whats-the-difference/

Memsource. (2020, February 2). *Roukaraizeishon ga groubarubijinesuni fukaketsunariyuu. [The reason why localization is essential for global businesses].* Retrieved March 24, 2022 from https://www.memsource.com/ja/blog/ja_why-localization-is-essential-for-global-business/

Your Writing

Globalization の3つの advantage か disadvantage について、480 words から 520 words で5パラグラフのエッセイを書きましょう。

Topic: Globalization
Thesis statement: There are three main advantages of globalization.
　　　　　　　　　(There are three main disadvantages of globalization.)
　　　　　　　　　(There are both advantages of disadvantages of globalization.)

5つの パラグラフの形と構成

エッセイの形にはいろいろなスタイルがありますが、ここでは、American Psychological Association (APA) style を使います（詳しくは Appendix の「引用・参考文献の書き方」を参照→p. 117）。

どのパラグラフも初めは、3文字（または5文字）引っ込めます。

Introduction （news, examples, history などの background information を書く）
Thesis statement

The first advantage is ～ .
Supporting sentences (examples, survey data, opinions from experts, etc.)

The second advantage is ～ .
Supporting sentences (examples, survey data, opinions from experts, etc.)

The third advantage is ～ .
Supporting sentences (examples, survey data, opinions from experts, etc.)

In conclusion, thesis statement の言い換え
　　　　　　3つの advantages を繰り返す
　　　　　　Concluding sentence

IV Grammar for Writing

A）注意！　日本語のメリットとデメリットは英語では advantages and disadvantages。 merits and demerits ではない。

Example sentences:

There are advantages and disadvantages of globalization.

Being well-known gives the product an advantage over other products.

B）つなぎ言葉 (transitional words) を使って書いてみよう！（ここでは副詞・副詞句を扱います）

Additional information:

furthermore, moreover, in addition, additionally

Intensified information:

in fact, as a matter of fact

Restatements:

in other words, in short

Examples:

for example, for instance

Consequences:

as a result, consequently

Cause:

because (of), due to, as a result (of),

Contrasting information:

however, although, even though, nevertheless, nonetheless, on the other hand

Order:

first/second/third, etc. (firstly, secondly, thirdly), then, next, last, finally

Conclusion:

in short, to conclude, in conclusion, in summary, to sum up

Exercise　（→p. 122 参照）

Unit 6

Global organizations

Can Do

Structure: 説明や解説のエッセイで、分類の書き方を知る。
Content: 世界的な機関について知り、説明することができる。

S: 物事を分類して説明する書き方を学びます。

C: 国際問題を学ぶ時、国連に代表される国際機関に関して知ることは必須です。
それらの起源、目的、社会の出来事との関連を学びます。

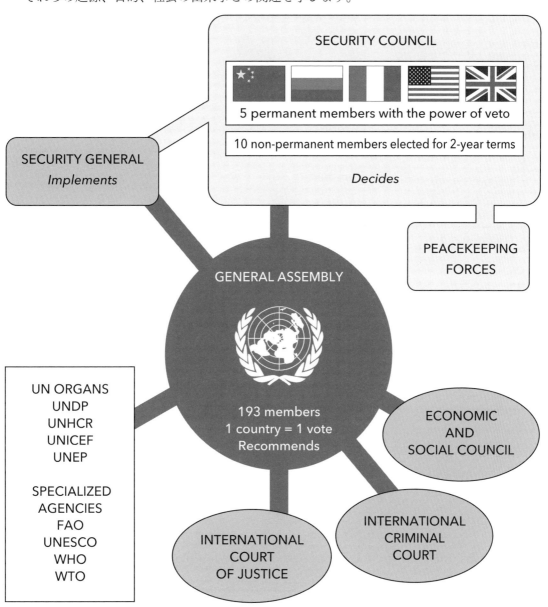

SECURITY COUNCIL

5 permanent members with the power of veto

10 non-permanent members elected for 2-year terms

SECURITY GENERAL
Implements

Decides

PEACEKEEPING
FORCES

GENERAL ASSEMBLY

193 members
1 country = 1 vote
Recommends

UN ORGANS
UNDP
UNHCR
UNICEF
UNEP

SPECIALIZED
AGENCIES
FAO
UNESCO
WHO
WTO

ECONOMIC
AND
SOCIAL COUNCIL

INTERNATIONAL
COURT
OF JUSTICE

INTERNATIONAL
CRIMINAL
COURT

I　Expository paragraphs: Classification

ある事柄を説明（解説）するパラグラフを expository paragraphs と呼びます。

A) ここでは、「分類」をとりあげます。この expository paragraphs は、coherence （首尾一貫）が大事で、ある論理や理由 (a principle) に基づき分類をします。

Example: Schools

	Principle	Schools
1	管轄	Public schools and private schools
2	性別	Boys' schools, girls' schools and co-education
3	年齢	Elementary schools, middle schools, high schools, and universities

Exercise: 国についての分類です。国の名前を入れましょう

	Principle	Countries
1	管轄	Europe (　　　) Asia (　　　) South America (　　　)
2	宗教(国民の多くが信仰している)	Christianity (　　　) Islam (　　　) Hindu (　　　) Buddhism (　　　)
3	大学生が行きたい国	

B) Organization of Classification (5パラグラフのエッセイの場合)

(Introduction=background information) （例：the UN の設立理由・最近の活動例/ニュース・主な組織等）
(Thesis statement)：The UN can be classified into several parts according to types of work. There are three well-known organizations.

The first organization is ～ (A is ～). It was founded ～ .

The second organization is ～ (B is ～).

The third organization is ～ （C is ～）.

In conclusion, three organizations in the UN are familiar to most people.
(Concluding sentences)

II Content

国際関係に関する問題を考える時、国際的な機関についての知識はかかせません。さらにここでは影響力のあるNGOの存在も考慮して、NGOまで含めて学習します。

A Topic Introduction: **Global organizations**

Each team will read about a different organization. Read the sentences for your organization and put them in the correct order. Write the numbers in the boxes. Number 1 is the topic sentence and is already in the correct place!

A. The United Nations (UN)

Disc1-25
25))

1 | The United Nations (UN) is an international organization which was established after World War II on October 24 1945. Japan joined on December 18 1956.

☐ **A.** The UN Security Council is mainly responsible for peace and security. Its permanent members are China, France, the Russian Federation, the United Kingdom, and the United States. There are also 10 non-permanent members.

☐ **B.** However, it cannot intervene in the domestic affairs of any state unless there is a threat to the peace, a breach of the peace, or an act of aggression.

☐ **C.** This UN Charter aims to promote better standards of life, develop friendly relations among nations, achieve international cooperation, and maintain peace and security.

☐ **D.** The UN now has 193 member states and all have equal status. They are united by the principles of the Charter of the United Nations.

Key terms

The United Nations (UN) 国際連合　UN Security Council 国連安全保障理事会　permanent members 常任理事国　non-permanent members 非常任理事国　intervene in 干渉する　domestic affairs 内政　a breach of the peace 治安破壊［罪］、治安妨害　an act of aggression 侵略［的］行為　UN Charter 国連憲章　promote better standards of より高水準の［水準の高い］〜を促進　equal status 平等な地位、対等の地位　the Charter of the United Nations 国際連合憲章

B. The World Bank, International Monetary Fund (IMF), and World Trade Organization (WTO)

Disc1-26
26))

1   The World Bank was established at the 1944 Bretton Woods Conference. It's original purpose was to rebuild the economies of Europe after World War II.

☐   **A.** The International Monetary Fund (IMF) was also created at the Bretton Woods Conference. It aims to ensure stable exchange rates and international payments. These enable countries to transact with each other.

☐   **B.** It also aims to settle trade disputes between countries before they become political or military conflict. This helps to ensure a more peaceful and prosperous world.

☐   **C.** It now provides loans and grants to the governments of developing economies. The bank aims to end extreme poverty and increase shared prosperity.

☐   **D.** Lastly, there is the World Trade Organization (WTO). In 2022, it had 164 member countries, accounting for about 98% of world trade. Its priority is for trade to flow smoothly and freely.

Key terms

World Bank 世界銀行　　the 1944 Bretton Woods Conference 1944年ブレトン・ウッズ会議（1944年7月に米ブレトン・ウッズで開かれた、連合軍側の44か国の代表による、第2次大戦後の国際通貨および金融秩序を定めた会議）　International Monetary Fund (IMF) 国際通貨基金　　exchange rates 為替レート　international payments 国際決済、国際送金　　transact with ～と取引などを行なう settle trade disputes 通商紛争を処理・解決する　　peaceful and prosperous world 平和で豊かな世界　　grants 補助金、貸付金　　developing economies 発展途上経済、発展しつつある経済 extreme poverty 極度の貧困　　shared prosperity 繁栄の共有　　World Trade Organization (WTO) 世界貿易機関　　accounting for ～の割合を占める

C. The World Health Organization (WHO)

Disc1-27
27))

1   The World Health Organization (WHO) was founded in 1948. WHO is the United Nations (UN) agency which is responsible for international public health.

☐   **A.** To carry out all of the above work, WHO relies on contributions from UN member states and private donors. In 2021-22, the Bill & Melinda Gates Foundation were among the largest contributors.

☐   **B.** As such, WHO coordinates the world's response to international health emergencies, for example the COVID-19 pandemic. It works in more than 150 locations globally.

☐   **C.** In this way, WHO supports the UN Sustainable Development Goals (SDGs), in particular SDG 3, "Ensure healthy lives and promote well-being for all at all ages".

D. In addition to global emergencies, WHO's priorities include <u>heart-disease</u> and cancer. WHO also leads <u>global efforts</u> to expand <u>universal health coverage</u>.

Key terms

World Health Organization (WHO) 世界保健機関　**agency** 機関　**public health** 公衆衛生　**contributions**（出資、財政、金融などの）貢献　**private donors** 個人献金者（からの民間資金）　**Bill & Melinda Gates Foundation** ビル＆メリンダ・ゲイツ財団　**coordinates the world's response** 世界の対応を調整する　**pandemic** 伝染病が全国（世界）的に広がる、汎流行の　**UN Sustainable Development Goals** 国連持続可能な開発目標　**heart-disease** 心臓病　**global efforts** 国際努力、グローバルな取り組み　**universal health coverage** ユニバーサル・ヘルス・カバレッジ（すべての人が、適切な健康増進、予防、治療、機能回復に関するサービスを、支払い可能な費用で受けられること）

D. Non-Governmental Organizations (NGOs)

Disc1-28　28))

1　In its simplest definition, a <u>non-governmental organization</u> (NGO) is a <u>non-profit</u> <u>humanitarian</u> organization that has not been established by the government.

A. In short, although there is some <u>criticism of</u> NGOs, their <u>role in global society</u> continues to increase. <u>World NGO Day</u>, which was recognized by the United Nations in 2014, is celebrated annually on February 27.

B. With this money and support, NGOs can <u>have a significant influence over</u> governments and companies by <u>lobbying</u>, reporting <u>bad business practices</u> in the media, or organizing <u>protests</u>.

C. While NGOs are normally <u>independent of</u> governments, many <u>work closely with</u> governments or international organizations such as the United Nations.

D. NGOs are <u>active in a range of issues</u>, such as stopping <u>human rights abuses</u> and protecting the environment. Many NGOs have <u>huge budgets</u> and memberships.

Key terms

non-governmental organization (NGO) 非政府組織　**non-profit** 非営利　**humanitarian** 人道主義の、人道主義的な　**criticism of** ～への批判、～に対する批判　**role in global society** グローバル社会における役割、国際社会における役割　**World NGO Day** 世界NGOデー（World NGO Dayは、2月27日に定められ、この日には世界各地でNGOに関する啓発活動が行われている）　**have a significant influence over** ～に大きな・重要な影響を与える　**lobbying** ロビーイング（非政府組織などが、政策や政治的判断を自分たちに有利な方向へ進んでいくようにするため、議会外の場で政治家に働きかけること）　**bad business practices** 無節操なビジネス慣行　**protests** デモ、抗議　**independent of** ～から独立している　**work closely with** ～と緊密に連携・協力する　**active in a range of issues** 幅広い社会問題に意欲的に取り組んでいる　**human rights abuses** 人権侵害　**huge budgets** 莫大な予算

Expert Presenters

You will make new teams, each with a student form a different organization. You will explain about your organization. First, prepare **the key points** that you want to explain. Be sure to take notes and don't forget to use 'Language for Learning' expressions (see page 6).

III **Writing Task:** Research and write about three organizations.

国連内外の組織、または、NGOをある基準を決め、3つ選んで説明しましょう。
まず、次の英文構造を確認します。英文を読んで、質問に答えましょう。

Writing: Classification

Three familiar organizations in the UN

Disc1-29
29 》)

The United Nations (UN) is the largest organization dedicated to international peace and relations in the world. It has a variety of specific organizations but can be classified into six major divisions: the General Assembly, Security Council, Economic and Social Council, International Court of Justice, Trusteeship Council,
5 and the UN Secretariat. Among these, the ones we often hear about are the General Assembly, Security Council, and Economic and Social Council.

The General Assembly is the division that makes decisions on UN policies. All member nations have one equal vote, regardless of their economic strength or population. Issues relating to peace, security, new membership admission, and
10 budget require a two-thirds vote. The assembly meets at UN headquarters. They also have a yearly conference in September, a special conference, and, if needed, an emergency conference. As an example, the policy of SDGs was adopted by the General Assembly in 2015.

The Security Council is the division responsible for peace and security under
15 the UN Charter. It consists of five permanent-member countries (China, France, Russia, the UK, and the US) and 10 non-permanent countries accepted by the General Assembly. The term of office for non-permanent countries is two years. The five permanent-member countries have the power to veto any resolution. Emergency meetings were held to criticize missile launches by North Korea and
20 the Ukraine crisis in 2022.

The Economic and Social Council conducts surveys and does research on international issues other than politics, such as women's rights, population and youth, drugs, food, and crime. There are 54 member countries with a three-year-

term who report the results and make recommendations. However, since their
25 activities cover various fields, they set up a lot of committees and cooperate
with specialized agencies such as UNESCO, FAO, and WHO. Because of the
diverse nature of their activities, policymakers, assembly members, academics,
foundations, businesspeople, young people, and NGOs are all involved in the
decision-making process.

30 In conclusion, the UN has six major divisions, the most familiar being the
General Assembly, Security Council, and Economic and Social Council. In addition
to the other three divisions, these were established to help all people, everywhere
in the world. Although there is some criticism of its limited power, especially in the
area of war, the UN is an important organization that is crucial to helping maintain
35 peaceful relations in the world.

Bibliography

U.N. Information Center. (n.d.). *Soukai [General Assembly]*. Retrieved March 21, 2022 from
   Marrhttps://www.unic.or.jp/info/un/un_organization/ga/

U.N. Information Center. (n.d.). *Anzenhoshourijikai [Security Council]*. Retrieved March 21, 2022 from
   https://www.unic.or.jp/info/un/un_organization/sc/

Volunteer Platform. (n.d.). *Kokurennkeizaishakairijikai [United Nations Economic and Social Council/
   ECOSOC]*. Retrieved March 23, 2022 from https://volunteer-platform.org/words/academic-terms/
   united-nations-economic-and-social-council/

Key terms

General Assembly 総会   Security Council 安全保障理事会   Economic and Social Council
経済社会理事会   International Court of Justice 国際司法裁判所   Trusteeship Council
信託統治理事会   UNESCO (the United Nations Education, Scientific and Cultural
Organization) ユネスコ（国連教育科学文化機関）   FAO (Food and Agriculture Organization) 食
糧農業機関

Question 1: The thesis statement に波線を引きましょう。

Question 2: 3つの機関があがっていますが、3つに共通する基準はなんですか？

Question 3: 次の表に説明を入れて、完成させましょう。

The UN	Field	Role	Member	Features	Examples of Activities
General Assembly					
Security Council					
Economic and Social Council					

Your Writing

5パラグラフのエッセイを書きましょう。国連、その他の機関、NGOなどをある基準で分け、そのうちの3つについて説明をします。1パラグラフ、100 wordsをめざして5パラグラフのエッセイを書いてみましょう。

 IV   Grammar for Writing

A) Classificationの表現

1. NGOs <u>can be divided into</u> at least five types by field; peace, education, medical, human rights, and the environment.
2. Governments <u>can be classified into</u> eight types; democracy, communism, socialism, oligarchy, aristocracy, monarchy, theocracy, and colonialism.

B) 分類に制限をかける表現

1. There are three reasons countries have nuclear weapons.
2. There are three types of politicians in this election.
3. Permanent and non-permanent members are the two types of membership in the Security Council.

C) 前置詞・前置詞句 (The UNのエッセイから)

1. <u>regardless of</u> their economic strength or population.
2. <u>under</u> the UN Charter
3. responsibility <u>for</u> peace and security
4. research <u>on</u> international issues
5. <u>Because of</u> (Due to) the nature of these activities, ~
6. <u>In addition to</u> two other organizations, ~
7. <u>In the case of</u> wars, ~

Exercise　(→p. 123参照)

The United Nations' Sustainable Development Goals

Can Do
Structure: 物事の経過・順（プロセス）を意識し、説明や解説のエッセイが書ける。
Content: SDGsについて知り、説明できる。

S: プロセスを入れながら、物事の説明や解説が書けるようにします。
C: SDGsについて基本的な事柄を学習し、その取り組みについて説明できるようにします。

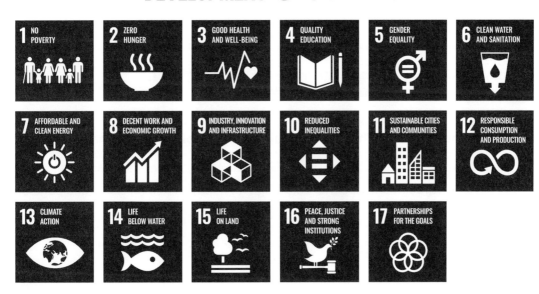

I　Expository paragraphs: Process

A) 経過を書く

この章では、SDGsの取り組みについて論理的に説明するエッセイを書きますが、特にどのような経過をたどって、その取り組みが行われたかというプロセスを部分的に意識して書きます。つまり、行為のプロセスを、順序だてて段階を追って説明するので、narrative paragraphs の chronological ordering の要素も入ってきます。

B) Organization

1. 5つのパラグラフエッセイの場合

> Introduction (news, examples, history, situation, etc.)
> Thesis statement: There are several thought-provoking projects conducted by companies.

> ABC company has engaged in ～ .

> XYZ Co., Ltd started a project ～ .

> Several companies cooperated with each other.

> Thus, several projects conducted by companies are inspiring.

II Content

2015年に国連で採択されてから、地球や人類を救う目標が掲げられました。それが、SDGsです。具体的にどのようなものなのか、基本的な事柄を学習します。

A Topic Introduction: **The UN Sustainable Development Goals (SDGs)**

Read the passage and answer the questions that follow. Share and check your answers with your team. Use the 'Language for Learning' expressions (see page 6).

1

Disc1-30

The UN Sustainable Development Goals (SDGs) were introduced at the United Nations Conference on Sustainable Development in Rio de Janeiro, Brazil, in 2012. They replace the Millennium Development Goals (MDGs), which started a global effort to tackle poverty in the year 2000. The SDGs commenced in 2015, and
5 the UN aims to achieve them by the year 2030.

The SDGs aim to tackle the most urgent environmental, political, and economic challenges facing our world today. For example, around the world, hundreds of millions of people still do not have enough food to eat. The wealth gap between rich and poor is widening. Women still earn less than men for the same
10 or similar work, and they have fewer rights. Moreover, human activity continues to have a devastating impact on the environment.

Question 1: When were the SDGs created, and what do they replace?
Question2: Which of the following is not described in the passage above?

a. poverty and hunger

b. access to education

c. gender inequality

d. climate change

Key terms

United Nations Conference on Sustainable Development 国連持続可能な開発会議
Millennium Development Goals (MDGs) ミレニアム開発目標　　tackle ～に取り組む　　urgent
... challenges 喫緊の課題　　face 直面する　　hundreds of millions of 数億の　　wealth gap 貧
富の格差　　earn 金を稼ぐ　　have a devastating impact on ～に計り知れない影響を与える、～を破
綻させる

2

To tackle such issues, all 193 United Nations (UN) member states agreed to 17 SDGs. These include, for example, good health and well-being; gender equality, decent work and economic growth; and sustainable cities and communities. The 17 goals are <u>interdependent</u>; that is, success in one goal affects success in another.
5 For instance, achieving gender equality (SDG 5) will lead to greater economic growth (SDG 8) as more women participate in the <u>workforce</u> and contribute to the country's GDP.

The UN SDGs are the most ambitious effort to improve the lives of all humanity. Yet, the ongoing <u>social and economic impacts</u> of COVID-19 are
10 threatening these goals. In both rich and poorer countries, COVID-19 has <u>negatively impacted</u> health and well-being; employment and income; access to education, and human rights. It has been especially <u>damaging to</u> the lives of women and girls. In this context, further global cooperation to <u>accelerate progress</u> towards achieving the SDGs is more important than ever.

Question 3: Which countries have agreed to the SDGs?

Question 4: How are the 17 SDGs <u>interdependent</u>? Explain.

Question 5: How has COVID-19 <u>negatively impacted</u> the SDGs?

Key terms

interdependent 相互依存的　　workforce 労働力　　GDP (Gross Domestic Product) 国内総生
産　　social and economic impacts 社会経済的影響　　negatively impacted 悪影響を受けた、悪
い影響を与えた　　damaging to 損害・被害を引き起こす　　accelerate progress 進展を加速させる、
進歩を促す

B | What exactly are the 17 SDGs?

The 17 SDGs are listed below in English and Japanese. Use the words in the box to complete the English SDGs.

justice	water	responsible	quality	partnerships
well-being	hunger	action	sustainable	equality	~~poverty~~
sanitation	clean	decent work	inequality	infrastructure	life

1. No _____poverty_____ 貧困をなくそう

2. Zero _____ 飢餓をゼロに

3. Good health and _____ すべての人に健康と福祉を

4. _____ education 質の高い教育をみんなに

5. Gender _____ ジェンダー平等を実現しよう

6. Clean water and _____ 安全な水とトイレを世界中に

7. Affordable and _____ energy エネルギーをみんなに そしてクリーンに

8. _____ and economic growth 働きがいも経済成長も

9. Industry, innovation and _____ 産業と技術革新の基盤をつくろう

10. Reduce _____ 人や国の不平等をなくそう

11. _____ cities and communities 住み続けられるまちづくりを

12. _____ consumption and production つくる責任 つかう責任

13. Climate _____ 気候変動に具体的な対策を

14. Life below _____ 海の豊かさを守ろう

15. _____ on land 陸の豊かさも守ろう

16. Peace and _____. Strong institutions 平和と公正をすべての人に

17. _____ for the goals パートナーシップで目標を達成しよう

C | Exploring connections between the 17 SDGs

The passage states that the "17 goals are interdependent", for example: "achieving gender equality (SDG 5) will lead to greater economic growth (SDG 8)". Which of the 17 SDGs do you think are most interdependent? Write three sentences describing the connections.

Useful Phrases

| "Achieving ~ " | "Ensuring ~ " |
| "~ will lead to ~ " | "~ will help to ~ " |

Example: "Achieving No poverty (SDG 1) or Zero hunger (SDG 2) will help to ensure Good health and well-being (SDG 3)."

- _____
  _____

- _____
  _____

- _____
  _____

III Writing Task: Research and write about projects related to the SDGs.

SDGsのプロジェクトについて調べ、その内容について（可能ならば途中プロセスも含め）説明をしてみましょう。
まず、次の英文構造を確認します。英文を読んで、質問に答えましょう。

SDG Projects by Corporations

(Disc1-32)
(32)))

Many projects have been launched in Japan since the 17 Sustainable Development Goals (SDGs) <u>were adopted by</u> the UN in 2015. A lot of international corporations have initiated projects as part of their <u>Corporate Social Responsibility (CSR)</u>. By <u>taking advantage of</u> their <u>resources</u>, they provide us with <u>concrete, thought-provoking</u> ideas.

Panasonic Corp., an electrical manufacturer, acted for SDG 1, "No Poverty." They launched a 100,000 <u>solar lanterns</u> project in 2013. By providing light to homes, schools, hospitals, roads, and stores, Panasonic has helped people in developing countries without electricity to recover from poverty. In 2018, their goal was met, yet this project has continued.

Nissin Foods Holdings Co., Ltd contributes to not only SDG 2, "Zero Hunger," but also to SDG 13, "Climate Action," SDG 14, "Life Below Water," and SDG 15, "Life on Land." In 2021, Nissin got rid of a plastic seal on their globally popular Cup

Noodle. The seal was used to close the lid for three minutes while the noodles
15　cooked in hot water. A paper holder was first used in 1984 but was changed to a
plastic holder in 2008. Since Cup Noodle sales were more than 100 billion yen in
2019, this small change reduced plastic waste by about 33 tons annually.

　　Some corporations have collaborated on their efforts. In 2021 for example,
Coca-Cola, Japan Inc. worked with UNIQLO, Ltd. on a campaign to win fleece
20　clothing made from recycled PET bottles to promote the idea of SDG 12,
"Responsible Consumption and Production." KOSE, Aeon Retail Co., Ltd., and
TerraCycle Inc. produced a shopping basket made from plastic marine waste.
Since 2021, this basket has been used at Aeon stores, to hold items for customers
while they shop. The aim of this campaign was to increase awareness of "Life Below
25　Water."

　　Thus, many corporations have acted in support of the UN SDGs. Since they
have a lot of resources such as <u>capital</u>, personnel, and facilities, they can work
toward achieving these goals effectively. Furthermore, since their products and
services are part of our daily lives, their actions help raise our awareness of these
30　goals. Working together, these corporations have played an important role in
helping to save the earth, fight climate change, and reduce waste.

Bibliography

Eguchi Holding Groups. (n.d.) *SDGs Nisshinshokuhinnno aratana chosenn [Nisshin Foods Co.'s New Challenge]*. Retrieved March 6, 2022 from https://eguchi-hd.co.jp/resolabo-sdgs-cup-noodle/

SDG Entrepreneurs (2021, February 21). *Kigyou no SDGs jissenjirei [Companies' SDGs projects]*. Retrieved March 8, 2022 from https://sdgsjapan.com/day30

TRANS. (2021, September 28). *KigyounoSDGsno Torikumijirei 15 sen [15 SDGs projects by corporations]*. Retrieved March 8, 2022 from https://www.trans.co.jp/column/sdgs/sdgscase2021/

Key terms

be adopted by 採択される　　**Corporate Social Responsibility (CSR)** 企業の社会的責任
take advantage of うまく利用する　　**resources** 資源　　**concrete** 具体的な
thought-provoking 示唆に富む、興味をそそる　　**solar lantern** 太陽光発電のランタン
capital 資本［金］

Question 1: The thesis statement に波線を引きましょう。

Question 2: 企業がSDGsに貢献するのは、どのような考えが元になっているのでしょうか？　その言葉に[　　]を付けましょう。

Question 3: エッセイの内容を整理するために、次の表を埋めましょう。

	Companies	Goal	Year	Actions
1	Panasonic Corp.	"No Poverty"	2013 ~	Provided 100,000 solar lanterns
2	Nisshin Foods Holdings Co., Ltd			
3	Coca-Cola Bottlers Japan Inc. UNIQLO Co., Ltd			
4	KOSE, Aeon Retail Co., Ltd. and TerraCycle Inc.			

Your Writing

SDGsを目指した3つのプロジェクトに関して、5パラグラフのエッセイを書きましょう。
日本か海外か、また、自治体、企業、学校（またはその協働）を選択し、1パラグラフ100
wordsをめざして書いてみましょう。

Ⅳ　Grammar for Writing

A)「(ゴール)を目指す」という表現
目指す
aim for the goal
aim to increase awareness of "Life Below Water"
aim to become a researcher
aim for the reduction of
work towards achieving that goal
実現する
achieve a goal
realize a goal

B) 年代順、日付順の結合語　(Chronological connectors)
つなぎ言葉：first, second, third, next, finally, after that
接続詞：and, after, before, since, when, while
前置詞：after, before, in addition to, prior to, since

Exercise　次の文章に適切な結合語を選び空所に入れましょう。

SDG Projects by Corporations
　　　Many concrete, thought-provoking projects have been launched by Japanese corporations [1](　　　　) SDGs were adopted by the UN in 2015. Their actions have been considered part of their CSR, Corporate Social Responsibility. For example,
5　Panasonic Corp. started their 100,000 solar lanterns project in 2013 and achieved that goal in 2018. However, even [2](　　　　), they have continued this project. In 2021, Nissin Foods Co., Ltd reduced their use of plastics for their popular Cup Noodle by eliminating a plastic seal used to hold the lid while the noodles cooked in hot water. Corporations have also collaborated on projects. Coca-Cola, Japan
10　Inc. worked with UNIQLO, Ltd. [3](　　　　) launched a campaign to win fleece clothing made from recycled PET bottles. [4](　　　　), KOSE, Aeon Retail Co., Ltd., and TerraCycle Inc. produced a shopping basket made from plastic marine waste. It is used in supermarkets to hold products [5](　　　　) customers pay. Thus, various corporations have worked to realize SDGs by taking advantage of
15　their resources.

after that	since	before	additionally	and

Unit 8 Human rights

Can Do
Structure: 比較のエッセイの構成を知る。一部定義も入れる。
Content: 人権について知る。

S: 類似点、相違点を挙げながら、エッセイを書けるようにします。
C: さまざまな人権の基本事項を学習します。

I Comparison and Contrast

A) 2つのものごとについて類似点を書く場合をcomparisonといい、相違点を書く場合をcontrastといいます。いずれの場合も、2つのものごとは、1) 同じ種類で、2) 同じ基準で比べます。

1) 同じ種類：
   ○ アメリカのLGBTQ＋の権利　vs　日本のLGBTQ＋の権利
   × アメリカの女性の権利　　　　vs　日本のLGBTQ+の権利

2) 同じ基準
   ○ アメリカの同性カップルの結婚と子供　vs　日本の同性カップルの結婚と子供
   ○ アメリカの法律　　　　　　　　　　vs　日本の法律
   × アメリカの同性カップルの結婚と子供　vs　日本の異性カップルの結婚と子供
   × アメリカの医療の事情　　　　　　　vs　日本の里親制度の事情

B) エッセイの構成には３つのパターンがあります。

Basic Block Style

このスタイルは、比較しているものの類似点を書くパラグラフと相違点を書くパラグラフがあります。

Introductory paragraph: Thesis statement
Body paragraph 1: Compare A and B
Body paragraph 2: Contrast A and B
Concluding paragraph

Block Style

このスタイルは、比較しているものを１つずつ各パラグラフで説明していくもので、２つ目のものは、前のものを意識して説明します。

Introductory paragraph: Thesis statement
Body paragraph 1: Points about A
Body paragraph 2: Compare and/or Contrast B in relation to A
Concluding paragraph

Point-by-point Style

このスタイルのエッセイは、どの側面を比べているのかという項目に関して、パラグラフごとに説明していくものです。したがって、あるものごとの側面は３つとは限らないのですが、ここでは代表的な形として３つの側面を書きます。

Introductory paragraph: Thesis statement
Body paragraph 1: Point 1: Compare or Contrast A and B
Body paragraph 2: Point 2: Compare or Contrast A and B
Body paragraph 3: Point 3: Compare or Contrast A and B
Concluding paragraph

さまざまな人権についての基本事項、歴史的な背景などを学習します。

A Topic Comprehension: **Human rights (SDGs)**

Working in teams of four, each student will read one of the paragraphs by themselves and make notes, summarizing the key points.

1

The term *human rights* is connected to the establishment of the United Nations (UN) in 1945, and the Universal Declaration of Human Rights in 1948. But what exactly are human rights? There are four characteristics which define them. First, human rights are a demand for the creation and distribution of power, 5 wealth, and other human goods. Next, they must be something fundamental to life, not something non-essential like a larger house or newer smartphone. Third, the rights of an individual or a particular group must not threaten or exceed the rights of others. Finally, they should be equally possessed by all human beings.

Key terms

human rights 人権（国際連合では人権を「人種、性、国籍、民族、言語、宗教、社会的地位にかかわらず、生まれながらにして認められるべき権利」と定義している）　Universal Declaration of Human Rights 世界人権宣言　distribution 分配、配分　human goods ヒューマングッズ（繁栄し、幸せな人間の生活に不可欠なもの。例えば、人生、家族、友情、仕事と遊び、美しさ、知識など）　threaten 脅かす　exceed 超える　equally possessed 平等に所有される

2

Various kinds of human rights have developed over the last century. The first kind are presented in the International Covenant on Economic, Social and Cultural Rights, which was adopted by the UN in 1966. This covenant became law on January 3, 1976, and currently 171 states have committed to these rights. These 5 rights are a response to the historical exploitation of workers and colonial peoples. Examples of these rights are the right to work and leisure, the right to social security, the right to education, and the right to cultural freedom and scientific progress.

Key terms

International Covenant on Economic, Social and Cultural Rights 経済的・社会的・文化的権利に関する国際規約　adopted by 採択された　covenant 規約　committed to ～を批准した　exploitation of workers 労働者の搾取　colonial peoples 植民地の人民　social security 社会保障（病気や失業などで生活に困らないように支援するのが社会保障の制度）　scientific progress 科学進歩

3

Other kinds of human rights are described in the <u>International Covenant on Civil and Political Rights</u>, which was created by the UN in 1966. It became law on March 23, 1976. To date, 173 states have <u>committed to</u> respecting rights of this <u>covenant</u>. Some examples of these rights are <u>the right to life</u>, freedom from
5 discrimination, freedom of speech, freedom of religion, and <u>electoral rights</u>. <u>NGOs</u> like <u>Amnesty International</u> and <u>Human Rights Watch</u> have significantly <u>raised public awareness</u> of <u>human rights abuses</u> in such areas.

Key terms

International Covenant on Civil and Political Rights 市民的・政治的権利に関する国際規約
committed to ～を批准した　**covenant** 規約　**the right to life** 生存権　**electoral rights** 投票
権、選挙権　**NGOs (non-governmental organizations)** 非政府組織　**Amnesty International**
アムネスティ・インターナショナル（1961年に発足した世界最大の国際人権NGO）　**Human Rights**
Watch ヒューマンライツウオッチ（1978年に発足した米国ニューヨーク市に本部を置く世界最大級の人権NGO）
raised public awareness 世論の意識を向上させる、一般社会・国民などの認識を高める
human rights abuses 人権侵害

4

Over the past 60 years, the UN has created numerous human rights laws. However, the importance of human rights varies according to each country's own customs, culture, and <u>political agenda</u>. As such, not all countries have <u>adopted these laws</u>. China <u>has not ratified</u> the International Covenant on Civil and Political
5 Rights. The United States has not committed to the <u>International Covenant on Economic, Social and Cultural Rights</u>. Moreover, these are two of the world's most powerful countries, yet each has been accused of <u>human rights abuses</u>. In spite of globalization, <u>international consensus</u> on human rights seems <u>far from reach</u>.

Key terms

political agenda 政治課題、政治的目標　**adopted these laws** 法案を可決する　**has not**
ratified 批准しなかった　**International Covenant on Civil and Political Rights** 市民的・政治
的権利に関する国際規約　**International Covenant on Economic, Social and Cultural Rights**
経済的・社会的・文化的権利に関する国際規約　**human rights abuses** 人権侵害　**international**
consensus 国際合意　**far from reach** 成し遂げられない、達成不可能な

B **Three-Step Interview: Understanding Human Rights**

In pairs, share your summary with another student in your team. Listen and take notes carefully. Then, return together as a team of four and take turns to share what you learnt from your partner! In this way, you'll learn all four summaries. Don't forget to use the 'Language for Learning' expressions (see page 6)!

C   Three-Step Discussion

First, prepare your ideas about the topic in Japanese. Share and develop your ideas with your home team and then write out an opinion in English. Make new groups and share/discuss your ideas in English. Be sure to use your 'Language for Learning' and 'Discussion Phrases' (see page 6).

Since the COVID-19 pandemic, some countries require people in particular jobs (e.g., hospital workers and truck drivers) to get a vaccination. In your view, is it a human right to refuse the vaccination? Or, do you think that social responsibility is more important?

Example responses:
"I believe social responsibility is more important than an individual right. If you refuse the COVID-19 vaccination, you're putting everyone's lives at risk."

"I completely disagree that people must get vaccinated. Some people refuse vaccinations for religious reasons, and freedom of religion is a fundamental human right."

III   Writing Task: Research and write about several aspects of human rights.

Comparison and Contrast の3つの style のうち1つを選んで、エッセイを書きましょう。
まず、次の英文構造を確認します。英文を読んで、質問に答えましょう。

Living as LGBTQ+ in Japan and the US

 Disc2-5 / 37 »

Compared to the US, LGBTQ+ progress in Japan lags far behind. Sadly, however, LGBTQ+ people in the US still experience discrimination. A 2018 study by Voices of Youth Count* found that LGBTQ+ youth were 120% more likely to become homeless than heterosexual youth (Voices of Youth Count, 2018).
5 Additionally, a 2021 report by the Trevor Project* found that 54% of LGBTQ+ people had experienced some type of discrimination within the past year (The Trevor Project, 2021). Many Japanese LGBTQ+ people have had similar experiences. Thus, there are similarities as well as differences regarding LGBTQ+ people living in Japan and the US.
10   In terms of similarities, there are two major ones. First, many LGBTQ+ people in both countries hide their sexual identities. In 2020, the Center for American Progress reported that more than 50% of LGBTQ+ people hid their personal relationships to avoid discrimination (Gruberg, Mahowald, & Halpin,

2020). A survey by au Jibun Bank Corp. that same year also found that more than
15 80% of those interviewed were not "out" at work (au Jibun Bank, 2020). Secondly, in both Japan and the US, LGBTQ+ people, especially those who are transgender, have difficulty using public restrooms. In most places, public restrooms are still separated by gender. A transgender woman from the US said she "got stared at, spat at, and shouted at" whenever she tried to use a ladies' restroom." (Thorn, 2016).

20 Despite these similarities, there are also differences for LGBTQ+ people in Japan and the US. A major one is that same-sex marriage is legal in the US. This was established in 2015 by the US Supreme Court, which ordered all states to follow the law. During that same year, more than 390,000 same-sex couples were married in the US (Nikkei, 2015). On the other hand, there is no law allowing
25 same-sex marriage in Japan. Since 2015, Setagaya and Shibuya wards have issued partnership certificates for same-sex couples, which apply to public rental housing and also recognize them as family members at hospitals. However, since they are not recognized under law, Japanese same-sex partners have no right of inheritance or tax benefits. In 2020, under this system, only about 1300 same-sex couples
30 obtained partnership certificates, a big difference from same-sex unions in the US (Nippon.com, 2020).

Thus, there are similarities and differences between the LGBTQ+ experiences in Japan and the US. Even though the situation of LGBTQ+ in Japan is behind that of the US, both countries have similar experiences in terms of unfair treatment.
35 This highlights the importance of the UN's SDG 10 which encourages us to be more accepting of LGBTQ+ everywhere, and create a society where everyone can live peacefully, happily, and without discrimination.

---

*Notes:
Voices of Youth Count
- a nonprofit focused on helping homeless LGBTQ+ youth
  a national policy research initiative in the US
The Trevor Project
- a nonprofit focused on suicide prevention for LGBTQ+ youth
  Take action to protect transgender and nonbinary young people in Texas.
The Center for American Progress
- a public policy research and advocacy organization (a think tank)

References
au Jibun Bank. (2020, November 5). *LGBTQ no hachiwari ijyou ga shokubade kamingu auto shiteinai? Kigyou no LGBT shien seido no seibi jyoukyou ha? [Is more than 80 percent of LGBTQ not 'out' at work? Is there any system to support LGBT at corporations?]*. Retrieved March 10, 2022 from https://www.jibunbank.co.jp/column/article/00276/
Gruberg, S., Mahowald, L. & Halpin, J., (2020, October 6). *The State of LGBTQ Community in 2020*. The

Center for American Progress. Retrieved March 22, 2022 from https://www.americanprogress.org/article/state-lgbtq-community-2020/

Nikkei. (2015, July 2). *Douseikon zennbeidegouhou saikousai "kinnshino shuuhouha ikenn"[Same-sex marriage is legal in the U.S. and the Supreme Court said that the state law restricting it is illegal]*. Retrieved March 20, 2022 from

https://www.nikkei.com/article/DGXLASGM26H9N_W5A620C1MM8000/

Nippon.com. (2020, November 9). *Zenkokude 1301kumino douseikappuruni shoumeisho: partnershipseido sutatokara gonenn [1301 couples got a partnership certificate five years since the system started]*. Retrieved March 20, 2022 from https://www.nippon.com/ja/japan-data/h00860/

The Trevor Project. (2021). *National Survey on LGBTQ Youth*. Retrieved March 24, 2022 from https://www.thetrevorproject.org/wp-content/uploads/2021/05/The-Trevor-Project-National-Survey-Results

Thorn, R. (2016, June 8). *Why toilets are battleground for transgender rights?* BBC. Retrieved March 12, 2022 from https://www.bbc.com/news/uk-england-36395646-2021.pdf

Voices of Youth Count. (2018, April). *Missed Opportunities: LGBTQ Youth Homelessness in America*. Retrieved March 13, 2022 from https://voicesofyouthcount.org/wp-content/uploads/2018/05/VoYC-LGBTQ-Brief-Chapin-Hall-2018.pdf

---

Key terms

LGBTQ+ L（Lesbian レズビアン：女性同性愛者）、G（Gay ゲイ：(男性) 同性愛者）、B（Bisexual バイセクシュアル：両性愛者）、T（Transgender トランスジェンダー：身体の性別と性自認が異なる人）、Q（Queer クィア：異性愛を規範とする社会に違和感を覚える性的指向の人、またはQuestioning クエスチョニング：自己のジェンダーや性的指向を探している状態の人）、+（Plus：性の多様性の取りこぼしがないこと） **heterosexual** 異性愛者　**transgender woman** 男性として生まれ、性自認が女性の人　**stared at** にらまれる　**spat at** つばをはかれる　**same-sex marriage** 同性婚　**certificates** 証書　**public rental housing** 公営賃貸住宅　**right of inheritance** 相続権　**tax benefits** 税の優遇

Question 1: Which style of essay is this?

Question 2: Underline the thesis statement.

Question 3: What similarities and differences are in this essay? Fill in the blanks.

（→p.124 参照）

Your Writing

1. 3つの比較の style のうちの1つを選びましょう。
2. 日本ともう1つ別の国についての Human Rights を比べましょう。
3. トピックは、LGBTQ+, people with disabilities, children, the elderly, people with rare diseases, immigrants, religious minorities, racial minorities, etc.（Gender Gap は次のユニットで扱います）
4. 1パラグラフ、最低100 words 前後で、style により、4パラグラフか5パラグフ書きましょう。

Ⅳ Grammar for Writing

A) Comparison and Contrast (詳しくは、Unit 9)

1. Similarities
   in both Japan and the US
2. Differences
   however,
   on the other hand,
   Unlike the US,

B) Reporting words

A 2017 study by Voices of Youth Count found that ～
According to a 2021 report by the Trevor Project,
In 2020, the Center for American Progress reported that ～

表現	意味
Some people claim that ～ .	ある人々は主張する（他の人は違うと言うかもしれない・証明されていないが）
Professor Sato argues that ～ .	佐藤教授は反論する 　　　　　説得する
A politician asserts that ～ .	ある政治家は明確に断固として主張する
A researcher maintains that ～ .	ある研究者は主張をつらぬく

Exercise　（→p. 124 参照）

Unit 9 Gender inequality

Can Do
Structure: 比較のエッセイの構成を知る。
Content: ２つの国の、男女の性別による格差を説明する。

S: 比較の構成について学びます。
C: 男女格差についてのレポートを読み、2つの国の状況を説明しましょう。

I Comparison and Contrast

2つの物事を比べる時、類似点を述べることをcomparisonと言い、相違点を述べることを
contrastと言います。

A) 比べる時に大事なことが２点あります。

1. 同じ種類のものごとを比較、対比する。
   例えば、ニューヨークと日本を比べるのではなく、ニューヨークと東京を比べる。
2. 同じ基準で比較、対比する。
   ニューヨークでの女性会社経営者の数と東京の女性政治家の数を比べるのではなく、
   ニューヨークの女性会社経営者と東京の女性会社経営者の数を比べる。

B) エッセイの構成には３つのパターンがあります。(See Unit 8.)

ここでは、Point-by-point Styleのスタイルだけもう一度見直します。

Point-by-point Style

このスタイルのエッセイは、どの側面を比べているのかという項目に関して、パラグラフごとに説明していくものです。したがって、あるものごとの側面は3つとは限らないのですが、ここでは代表的な形として3つの側面を書くということで示します。

Introductory paragraph: Thesis statement
Body paragraph 1: Point 1: Compare or Contrast A and B
Body paragraph 2: Point 2: Compare or Contrast A and B
Body paragraph 3: Point 3: Compare or Contrast A and B
Concluding paragraph

II Content

男女格差についてのレポートが毎年報告されています。それを元に、日本と他の国の状況について理解します。

A Topic Comprehension: **Gender inequality**

In teams of four, two students read Passage A and two students read Passage B. Check that you understand the meaning of the passage and make notes about the key points. Be sure to use your 'Language for Learning' expressions (see page6).

Disc2-6

38))

Student A Reading Passage

Eradicating gender inequality is crucial for societies and economies to flourish. Since 2006, over 250 million more women have entered the global labor force. Yet, as of 2021, women across the world were earning on average 37% less pay than men for the same or similar work (World Economic Forum, 2021). Women's
5 jobs are also under threat. Due to automation and technological innovations, the number of manufacturing, retail, and service jobs for women will likely decline significantly in OECD countries (OECD, 2017).

Looking at Japan, an OECD country, some research suggests that greater economic gender equality could increase GDP by $408 billion (PwC, 2022), or
10 ¥53 trillion — a significant amount. Developing Japan's female talent will have a huge impact on the country's future growth and competitiveness. In facing this challenge, therefore, it is important to understand what exactly the gender gap is.

Key terms

eradicating gender inequality 男女不平等性をなくす、ジェンダー不平等をなくす   the global labor force 世界的な労働力、グローバルな労働力   earn お金を稼ぐ   under threat 失業の脅威にさらされる   automation オートメーション、自動化   decline 雇用の減少   OECD countries 経済協力開発機構諸国（OECD = Organization for Economic Cooperation and Development）   economic gender equality 経済活動の男女平等   GDP (= Gross Domestic Product) 国内総生産

Disc2-7
39)))

Student B Reading Passage

The Global Gender Gap Report was first published in 2006 by the World Economic Forum, an NPO, or Non-Profit Organization. The report aims to understand whether countries are distributing their resources and opportunities fairly between women and men. The report uses four indexes to measure gender
5 equality. The report then ranks countries from highest to lowest equality, which enables a comparison.

    1. Economic Participation and Opportunity – salaries, participation, and leadership

    2. Education – access to basic and higher levels of education

10   3. Political Empowerment – representation in governments

    4. Health and Survival – healthy life expectancy

The Global Gender Gap report 2021 ranked 156 countries. Japan ranked 120th, rising 1 place from the previous year. In terms of Economic Participation and Opportunity, the country ranks 117th. In spite of being one of the world's most
15 advanced economies, the proportion of time that women in Japan spend on unpaid domestic work is five times more than that of men (Budgen, 2021).

In Japan, as in many countries globally, much more needs to be done before women are able to live, work, and participate equally in society. To achieve this, governments, employers, and educators will all have a role to play.

Key terms

Non-Profit Organization (NPO) 非営利団体   distributing 分配する   index 指数   Political Empowerment 政治への関与   healthy life expectancy 健康寿命   unpaid domestic work 無給の家事労働   have a role to play ～において役割を有する

References

Budgen, M. (2021, June 21). Pandemic magnifies household gender roles in Japan. *The Japan Times*. Retrieved May 2, 2022 from https://www.japantimes.co.jp/news/2021/06/21/national/social-issues/women-work-gender-roles/

OECD. (2017, July 17). *Going digital: the future of work for women*. Retrieved May 2, 2022 from https://www.oecd.org/employment/Going-Digital-the-Future-of-Work-for-Women.pdf

PwC. (2022). *Women in Work Index 2022*. Retrieved May 2, 2022 from https://www.pwc.co.uk/services/economics/insights/women-in-work-index.html#dataexplorer

World Economic Forum. (2021, March 30). *Global Gender Gap Report 2021*. Retrieved May 2, 2022 from https://www3.weforum.org/docs/WEF_GGGR_2021.pdf

 B **Pair Oral Quiz**

Make new pairs so that there is one A Student and one B Student. Quiz your partner using the questions below.

Questions to ask Student A

Question 1: How many women have entered the global labor force since 2006?

A. Over 150 million

B. Over 200 million

C. Over 250 million

Question 2: On average how much less do women earn for the same or similar work as men?

A. 27%   B. 33%   C. 37%

Question 3: Why are women's jobs under threat?

Question 4: What can you tell me about retail, manufacturing and service jobs?

Question 5: What did you learn about the economic advantage of achieving gender equality in Japan?

Questions to ask Student B

Question 1: Who publishes the Global Gender Gap Report?

A. The World Bank

B. The World Economic Forum

C. The World Health Organization

Question 2: What does the report aim to understand?

A. The kind of educational opportunities that countries provide

B. The number of women entering the workforce

C. Whether countries are distributing resources and opportunities equally

Question 3: What do you know about how the report measures gender equality?

Question 4: How many countries did the report rank in 2021?

Question 5: What can you tell me about Japan's 2021 performance?

C Describing the Global Top 10 Rankings

Table 1 below shows the global top 10 rankings for the 2021 report. Use the expressions in Box 1 below to describe the rankings in two countries (e.g., Finland and Ireland) or two regions (e.g., Africa and Scandinavia). Then share them with your team.

Examples:
"In terms of the top country, Iceland's ranking remained unchanged in 2021."
"Regarding Norway, the country dropped one place in 2021 from 2nd to 3rd."
"Looking at the data on Africa, Namibia and Rwanda both rose in 2021."

Table 1
Global Gender Equality Rankings for the Top Ten Countries in the 2021 Report

2020		2021			2020		2021	
1	⇒	1	Iceland		12	↑	6	Namibia
3	↑	2	Finland		9	↑	7	Rwanda
2	↓	3	Norway		33	↑	8	Lithuania
6	↑	4	New Zealand		7	↓	9	Ireland
4	↓	5	Sweden		18	↑	10	Switzerland

Data Source: World Economic Forum

Box 1 **Describing Movements in Data**

Introducing Data:
Looking at the data on / In terms of / Regarding [Europe / Africa / the top three countries / etc.], ...

Describing Data:
[Iceland's] ranking remained unchanged / remained the same / in 2021.
[Finland] moved up / went up / rose / increased [one ranking / one place / from 4th to 3rd place] in 2021.
[Ireland] moved down / went down / dropped / decreased [two rankings / two places / from 7th to 9th place] in 2021.

FLUENCY CHALLENGE!
Take turns with a partner and challenge each other to describe as much data as you can in 30 seconds. Listen carefully and check each other's accuracy (language and information) by referring to Box 1 and Table 1.

Writing Task: Research and write about several aspects of the report.

Comparison and Contrast の３つの style のうち１つを選んで、エッセイを書きましょう。
まず、次の英文構造を確認します。英文を読んで、質問に答えましょう。

Contrasting Gender Equality in the US and Japan

Disc2-8
40))

   The Global Gender Gap Report has been published by the World Economic Forum in Switzerland since 2006 to explain gender equality around the world. In the 2021 report, which ranked 156 countries, Scandinavian countries were once again in the top five, not other advanced economies like the US and Japan
5 (World Economic Forum, 2021). In terms of political empowerment and economic participation and opportunity, the US and Japan rank lower as democratic countries. Furthermore, the two countries' contrasting ranks indicate that their situations are quite different.

   In terms of political empowerment in 2021, the US at 37th place (0.329) and
10 Japan at 147th (0.061) rank low as democratic countries, indicating a wide range between their ranks and different situations (World Economic Forum, 2021). The total percentage of female members in the US Congress and the Japanese Diet was about 30% and 9.9% respectively (Kanamori, 2021). It has been said that the US election system could be a cause of difficulty for women to become members of
15 Congress. In Japan, research on the obstacles against women becoming a member of the Diet reported that 58.8% of respondents mentioned lack of specialist knowledge, 47.8% the difficulty of balancing housework and childcare, 40.9% the lack of privacy, and 34.8% cited sexual harassment (Yuzuki, 2021).

   In terms of the economic participation and opportunity index, the work
20 environments of these two countries are also very different. The US ranks 30th at 0.75, and Japan ranks 120th at 0.6 (World Economic Forum, 2021). These rankings are calculated from salary gaps, the ratio of management positions, and the number of specialists and engineers. In regards to the percentage of female CEOs in domestic companies, it is estimated that the US stands at 25% and Japan at 12% (Sekai no
25 nyusu, 2021). Women in both countries experience difficulty having a career as well as a family and face discrimination in large organizations, often referred to as the 'glass ceiling.' However, research by the OECD in 2014 reported that Japanese men work the longest hours among the 34 OECD countries, while the US ranked 16th among these same countries (Ricoh Workstyle Lab, 2021). In terms of time spent
30 doing housework, unlike women in the US, which ranked 22nd, Japanese women ranked third, doing almost five times more housework than that of Japanese men.

In contrast, in 2018, Rinnai, a Japanese kitchen maker, studied 500 people from Japan, South Korea, the US, Germany, and Denmark and found that men in the US spent the most time doing housework (Rinnai News Release, 2018).

35　　In conclusion, the US and Japan ranked lower than expected as democratic and economically advanced countries, and their situations are very different as shown by the wide range of their rankings. However, in order to increase female political empowerment, various NPOs are supporting women by providing knowledge, skills, and even financial aid in both the US and Japan. Furthermore, in

40 Japan, many businesses and government offices are promoting workplace reforms. By increasing support systems like these, it is hoped that both countries will come closer to gender equality in the near future.

Question 1: The thesis statementに波線を引きましょう。

Question 2: 3つのstyleのうちのどれで書かれているかをペアで確認しましょう。

Question 3: 表を埋めて、エッセイの構造を明確にしましょう。（→ p.125 参照）

References

Kanamori, T. (2021, January 4). Amerika renpougikai no joseigiinsuu ga kakosaita 144 [The number of the US Congress women was the largest ever, 144]. Tokyo Shimbun. Retrieved February 10, 2022 from https://www.tokyo-np.co.jp/article/77984

Ricoh Workstyle Lab. (2021, June 29). Nihon no roudou jikann ha sekaiyori nagai [Is Japanese working hours longer in the world?]. RICOH JAPAN Corporation.　Retrieved February 7, 2022 from https://workstyle.ricoh.co.jp/article/workingtime.html

Rinnai News Release. (2018, February 8). Sekai gokakoku no tomobataraki ni kannsuru ishiki chousa [The survey on the attitude toward life of double-income families in five countries]. Rinnai. Retrieved February 8, 2022 from https://www.rinnai.co.jp/releases/2018/0208/

Sekai no nyusu. (2021, June 12). amerika no joseikeieisha ha nihonyori harukani ooinoka [Are there more female CEOs in the US than in Japan?].
Retrieved February 14, 2022 from https://www.thutmosev.com/archives/74151489.html

Shoji, K. (2019). Kolamu amerika deno torikumi [Column: measures in the US]. Gakushuin University.
Retrieved February 9, 2022 from https://www.gender.go.jp/research/kenkyu/pdf/gaikou_research/2020/11.pdf

World Economic Forum. (2021, March 30). The Global Gender Gap Report 2021. Retrieved February 13, 2022 from https://www.weforum.org/reports/ab6795a1-960c-42b2-b3d5-587eccda6023

Yuzuki, M. (2021, April 22). Joseigiinni naritakutemo…hansuuchikaku kaji・ikujito ryouritsukonnan de dannen naikakufuchousa [More than half of women said the difficulty of becoming a member of the Diet was balancing housework and childcare according to the research of the Cabinet]. Tokyo Shimbun.
Retrieved February 12, 2022 from https://www.tokyo-np.co.jp/article/99801

1. 3つの比較のstyleのうちの1つを選日ましょう（今回はすべて4パラグラフです）。
2. 日本ともう1つ別の国について、Global Gender Gap Reportの最新版と他の資料を使って比較を書きましょう。
3. Economic Participation and Opportunity, Educational Attainment, Health and Survival, とPolitical Empowermentの4つのポイントのうち2つについて比較しましょう。
4. 1パラグラフ、100 words前後から150〜160 wordsで書きましょう。

Ⅳ　Grammar for Writing

A) Comparisonの文章を書くときの表現

1. The US is one of the major economic powers in the world. <u>Also</u>, Japan is one of the major economic powers in the world.
   <u>Similarly</u>,
   <u>Likewise</u>,
2. The US is one of the major economic powers in the world <u>just as</u> Japan is.
3. <u>Both</u> the US <u>and</u> Japan are major economic powers in the world.
   <u>Not only</u> the US <u>but also</u> Japan is one of the major economic powers in the world.
   <u>Neither</u> the US <u>nor</u> Japan is ranked first in the list.
4. <u>Similar to</u> the US, Japan was ranked lower in the list.
   <u>Just like</u> the US, Japan was ranked lower in the list.
   <u>The same as</u> the US, Japan was ranked lower in the list.

B) Contrastの文章を書くときの表現

1. The US was ranked 37th; <u>however</u>, Japan was ranked 147th.
   The US was ranked 37th. Japan, however, was ranked 147th.
   The US was ranked 37th. In contrast, Japan was ranked 147th.
   <u>By contrast</u>,
   <u>On the other hand</u>,
   <u>However</u>,
   The US was ranked 37th, in contrast to Japan which was ranked 147th.
2. The US was ranked 37th, <u>while</u> Japan was ranked 147th.
   <u>whereas</u>
   The US was ranked 37th, <u>but</u> Japan was ranked 147th.
   <u>yet</u>
3. <u>Unlike</u> the US, Japan was ranked very low.
4. The US was ranked much <u>higher than</u> Japan.
   Japan was ranked much <u>lower than</u> the US.

Exercise　（→p. 126参照）

Terrorism

Can Do **Structure:** 分類のエッセイの構成を知る。
Content: テロとは何かを理解する。

S: 分類のエッセイの構成を知り、説明できるようにします。

C: テロとは何かを3つの側面（religious, ideological そして ethno-nationalist）という分類から理解します。

I Classification

A) 分類するということ

トピックに関する物事をグループ、カテゴリーに分け、それぞれについて例を出しながら説明していきます（See Unit 6）。ここでは、テロとはどういうことかを理解してから、さまざまなテロ組織についてある分類基準で分析してみます。

B) 分類の基準＝a principle

ここでは、religion, ideology, ethno-nationalism という3つの側面を考えます。もともとテロを分析しようとすると、たくさんの分析規準が考えられます。目的、international か domestic か、本拠地はどの国・地域か、宗教、主義主張や規則、支持を受けている国、

他のテロ組織との関係等があります。それらをすべて取り上げることはできないので、a principle を 3 つ選びます。

C) 区別の言葉

The first category is
The first type is
The first kind is
The first group is

D) Organization

いくつか分類したものに関しては、だいたい同じ数の例、同じ量の文章を書きます（ただし、分類が 2 つの場合は、全体が 4 パラグラフになります）。

> Introduction (news, history, example, etc.)
>
> Thesis statement: Terrorist groups can be classified into three categories.
> (The Taliban can be analyzed from three perspectives.)

> The first category is 〜 . （目的、メンバー、事例などを書いて説明する）

> The second category is 〜 . （目的、メンバー、事例などを書いて説明する）

> The third category is 〜 . （目的、メンバー、事例などを書いて説明する）

> In summary, ＋ restatement of the thesis statement
>
> Concluding sentences

ここで使えるつなぎ言葉（Transitions）
For example
For instance
Therefore
As a result
As a consequence
Consequently
For this reason

Content

世界にはさまざまなテロがありますが、まず、テロとは何かという基本的な事柄を学習します。

A Topic Introduction: **Terrorism**

Working with your team, read the paragraphs below and check you understand the meaning. Then choose the best summary sentence. Use the 'Language for Learning' phrases (see page 6).

 1

  Terrorism is a controversial and complex term. In its simplest definition, terrorism is the use of violence against the government, symbolic targets, or <u>civilians</u> to achieve political change. This political purpose distinguishes terrorist violence from <u>acts of criminal violence</u>. <u>Terrorist groups</u> have various motivations.

5 For example, in the 1970s <u>the Japanese Red Army</u> was motivated by <u>political ideology</u>, aiming to create <u>a Communist state</u> in Japan. Until 2018 in Spain, the group <u>ETA</u> was motivated by <u>ethnic nationalism</u>, using terrorism to try and <u>achieve an independent state</u>. Over the last 30 years, much terrorism around the world has been motivated by religion. <u>Al Qaeda</u> and <u>Islamic State</u> are two examples of

10 <u>Islamic terrorists</u> which want <u>to radically change</u> international society.

Summary Sentences

A. Terrorism is a complex term. The purpose of terrorism distinguishes it from other criminal violence. People commit terrorism for social and economic reasons.

B. Terrorism is violence against governments, symbolic targets, or civilians for political purposes. Terrorists can be motivated by ideology, ethnic nationalism, or religion.

Key terms

civilians 一般人、文民 acts of criminal violence 暴力犯罪、暴行罪 terrorist groups テロ組織 the Japanese Red Army 日本赤軍 political ideology 政治思想、イデオロギー
a Communist state 共産主義国 ETA (= Euzkadi ta Azktasuna) バスク祖国と自由
ethnic nationalism 民族主義 achieve an independent state 独立国家を樹立する
Al Qaeda アル・カーイダ Islamic State イスラム国、IS Islamic terrorists イスラム教のテロリスト to radically change 急進的に変化する

2

Terrorism is not a modern phenomenon. However, it was not until the 20th century that it developed into a major international concern. With the expansion of commercial air travel and TV news in the late 1960s, <u>hijackings</u> significantly increased. As a result, terrorists motivated by ideology and ethnic nationalism
5 <u>gained much publicity</u> on television. During the 1980s, terrorist attacks became more sophisticated and there was an increase in <u>suicide bombings</u>. By the 1990s, wars in the Middle East had led to <u>the emergence of</u> Islamic terrorists, most notably Al Qaeda. This group was later responsible for the <u>9/11 attacks</u> in the US, which killed 2,996 people. In 2003, some of Al Qaeda's members established a separate
10 terrorist group in Iraq, which later became the global terrorist group, Islamic State. While not as lethal as Islamic terrorism, a worrying trend in recent years is the rise of <u>far-right terrorism</u>, especially in <u>liberal democracies</u> such as the US and western European countries.

Summary Sentences

A. Terrorism increased from the 1960s. Islamic terrorism emerged in the 1990s and later became global. Recently, the West is experiencing a trend in far-right terrorism.

B. Terrorists can gain much publicity on TV and as a result the number of terrorist attacks have increased. Al Qaeda committed the September 11 attacks in the US.

Key terms

hijackings ハイジャック（不法に輸送機関の乗っ取りを行うこと） gained much publicity 知名度・認知度を非常に高める suicide bombings 自爆テロ、自爆攻撃（自分が爆弾を抱えて攻撃すること）
the emergence of ～の出現 9/11 attacks ９・11攻撃（2001年の米国同時多発テロは、９月11日に行われた） far-right terrorism (= right-wing terrorism) 右翼テロ（右翼イデオロギーを動機として引き起こされるテロリズムのこと） liberal democracies 自由民主主義

3

Whatever their motivation, all terrorists want to achieve some kind of political change. Seeking change in itself is acceptable. However, in modern, <u>civilized society</u>, using violence to achieve it is not. In liberal democracies, people with differing opinions and beliefs can normally participate actively and peacefully
5 in politics. Yet, that is not true in all countries. Due to <u>authoritarian governments</u>, <u>corrupt elections</u>, <u>state violence</u>, <u>exclusion</u>, and poverty, some citizens cannot change their circumstances through <u>the democratic process</u>. For some, the only option appears to be terrorism. The causes of terrorism are complex. As the world's peoples, cultures, and societies become more closely interconnected through
10 globalization, so too are the solutions.

Summary Sentences

A. There are three main reasons why citizens sometimes choose terrorism to change their circumstances. The causes of terrorism are complex. However, the solutions are also complex.

B. Using violence to achieve change is unacceptable. Yet, some citizens in terrible circumstances cannot makes changes through the democratic process. So, terrorism seems the only option.

Key terms

civilized society 文明社会   authoritarian governments 権威主義政府   corrupt elections 腐敗した選挙   state violence （国民に対する）国家的暴力   exclusion （政治的な）排除 the democratic process 民主的なプロセス、民主制度

(B)   **Pair Discussion**

The following discussion topics help you to develop your understanding about terrorism definitions and issues. In groups of four students, decide one or two questions you'd like to discuss.

1. Do you think that terrorism might affect Japan in the future? Give reasons and details.

2. The passage mentions that "authoritarian governments, corrupt elections, state violence, exclusion, and poverty" can lead some people to terrorism. Do you think that this justifies terrorism?

3. On January 6, 2021, a mob of about 2,500 supporters of the then US President Donald Trump attacked the Capitol Building in Washington, D.C. Why did they do it? Was this a kind of terrorism?

4. Why do you think far-right terrorism is increasing, especially in the US and some European countries?

III   **Writing Task: Research and write about terrorist organizations.**

下記の2つのやり方をどちらか選び、4パラグラフか5パラグラフのエッセイを書いてみましょう。

1. 1つの地域または国の中でのいくつかのテロ組織を、religious, ideological and ethno-nationalist を意識して説明しましょう。

2. 1つのテロ組織をとりあげ、religious なのか、ideological なのか、また ethno-nationalist なのかを説明しましょう（この中の2つでもよい）。

まず、次の英文構造を確認します。英文を読んで、質問に答えましょう。

The Taliban in Afghanistan

The Taliban is an Islamic fundamentalist group known for their harsh rules and abuse of human rights. Despite this, they returned to power in Afghanistan in 2021, after the stationing of US-led forces ended. Unfortunately, they immediately started killing politicians, policemen, journalists, or anyone closely related to the
5 former government. There is also concern that Afghanistan will now become a safe haven for terrorists (Gardner, 2021). In addition, due to the struggling economy, a lot of Afghans have tried to leave their country. In some ways, the nature of the Taliban over these past three decades has changed. This is an analysis from the perspectives of religion and ethno-nationalism.

10 As an organization, the Taliban was one of the most extreme and destructive who followed a strict religious ideology. They emerged from the Afghan War with the former Soviet Union (1978 to 1992) after the new government in Afghanistan failed to establish order and security. Around 1994, the group mainly consisted of former fighters associated with Islamic schools who strictly followed a fundamental
15 Islamic law. They began to capture and secure local areas, and by 1996 the Taliban had taken the capital city, Kabul, and were in control of most of the country. However, they faced severe resistance from other ethnic groups due to their strict religious ideology, laws, and brutal control of the population.

While fighting against the US and NATO forces at the beginning of the 21st
20 century, the Taliban's motivations can also be classified as ethno-nationalistic. After the 9/11 attacks on the US in 2001, the US started a war in Afghanistan. The goal was to kill Osama bin Laden, the leader of Al Qaeda, and prevent the Taliban from protecting him. During the conflict, resistance against the US-led forces increased and encouraged people to join both the Taliban and Al Qaeda, not
25 because of Islamic fundamentalist ideology, but because of anti-US sentiment. As a result, with the support of the general public, a large number of Taliban soldiers covered 60% of the country, spreading deep into the countryside and mountainous areas (Swiss Info, 2008). Thus, they could fight advantageously.

In conclusion, the various motivations of terrorism can often overlap,
30 depending on the circumstances. The Taliban was initially a religious fundamentalist group, but later adopted ethno-nationalism to fight against foreign influences. Some have considered the recent revival of the Taliban as a 'a global failure' of the western world. In any case, if the Taliban's goal is to create a new, sovereign-state system, it will be difficult for them to remain terrorists. Afghans are unlikely to
35 accept a terrorist group, even if they agree with its religious and ethno-nationalist beliefs. In order to succeed, they must stop killing people and begin cooperating

with existing political systems.

References

Gardner. F. (2021, August 17). *Afuganisutan wa terososhikino anzennchitaininarunoka tariban fukkennde [Does Afghanistan become a safe haven after the Taliban returned to power?]* BBC. Retrieved March 25, 2022 from https://www.bbc.com/japanese/features-and-analysis-58240280

Swiss Info. (2008, September 26). *Afuganisutann hisokana nationalism no taitou [Nationalism appeared secretly in Afghanistan].* Retrieved March 27, 2022 from https://www.swissinfo.ch/jpn/%E3%82%A2%E3%83%95%E3%82%AC%E3%83%8B%E3%82%B9%E3%82%BF%E3%83%B3-%E5%AF%86%E3%81%8B%E3%81%AA%E3%83%8A%E3%82%B7%E3%83%A7%E3%83%8A%E3%83%AA%E3%82%BA%E3%83%A0%E3%81%AE%E5%8F%B0%E9%A0%AD/6938544

Key terms

an Islamic fundamentalist group イスラム教原理主義派　　harsh rules 厳しい規則　　abuse 虐待、乱用、侵害　　stationing 駐在する　　a safe haven 安全地帯　　a struggling economy 低迷する経済　　perspectives 観点　　ethno-nationalism 民族主義　　extreme 過激　　destructive 破壊主義　　associated with 提携する、連合する　　NATO 北大西洋条約機構　　classified 区別される　　resistance 反対、抵抗　　anti-～sentiment 反感　　the general public 一般市民　　a failure 失敗　　a sovereign-state system 一主権国家

Question 1: The thesis statement に波線を引きましょう。

Question 2: なぜ、タリバンの国、アフガニスタンから国民が逃げようとしているのですか？　その理由を答えましょう。

Question 3: 歴史の変遷とタリバンの変化について表を完成させましょう。

The Taliban in Afghanistan

Historical Events	The Taliban in Afghanistan
The Afghan War with the Soviet Union (1978 to 1992)	
The Taliban's control over the country in 1996	
From 2001 to 2020: The fight against the US and NATO forces	

下記の2つのやり方をどちらか選び、4つか5つのパラグラフのエッセイを書いてみましょう。

1. 1つの地域または国の中でのテロ組織を、religious, ideological and ethno-nationalist を意識して説明しましょう。

2. 1つのテロ組織をとりあげ、religious なのか、ideological なのか、また ethno-nationalist なのかを説明しましょう（この中の2つでもよい）。

IV   Grammar for Writing

A) 分類の表現（詳しくはUnit 6）

1. Terrorist groups can be divided into three types.
   classified into five categories.
2. Terrorist groups can be analyzed from three perspectives; religion, ideology, and ethno-nationalism.
3. There are three categories of terrorism; religion, ideology, and ethno-nationalism.

B) 副詞の使い方: Adverb

一般動詞と組み合わせる時は、通常その動詞のすぐ後ろに置かれますが、基本的に文法的にはどこにでも置けます。

この副詞をうまく使えるようになると、自分の書きたい文章がより正確に表現できるようになります。

サンプル・エッセイの中の副詞

unfortunately,   immediately,   mainly,   strictly,
eventually,   initially,   unlikely,

Exercise   （→ p. 127参照）

International development

Can Do

Structure: 原因と結果のエッセイを書く。
Content: 開発、貧困、飢餓について知る。

S: 原因と結果についてのエッセイを書けるようにします。
C: 開発、貧困、飢餓について基本的な事柄、問題について学習し、説明できるようにします。

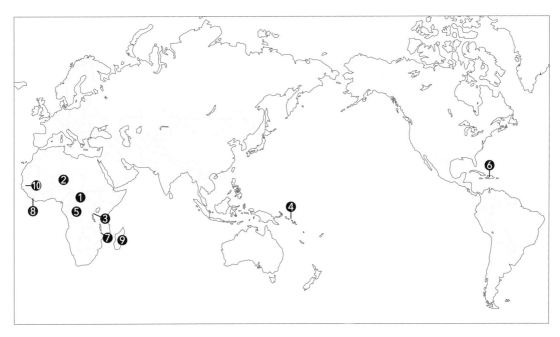

A List of the Top 10 Poorest Countries in the World 2022

❶ Central African Republic   中央アフリカ
❷ Niger   ニジェール
❸ Burundi   ブルンジ
❹ Solomon Islands   ソロモン諸島
❺ Democratic Republic of Congo   コンゴ民主共和国
❻ Haiti   ハイチ
❼ Malawi   マラウイ
❽ Liberia   リベリア
❾ Madagascar   マダガスカル
❿ Gambia   ガンビア

https://eafeed.com/a-list-of-top-10-poorest-countries-in-the-world-2020-2021/

I Cause and Effect

A) 原因と結果のエッセイには、大きくわけて２つの形があります。

1. 1つ目は、ある事柄があり、その原因をいくつか書く形

   Some African countries suffer from poverty.

   ↑   ↑   ↑

   Reason 1   Reason 2   Reason 3
   Civil wars   Drought   Diseases

2. 2つ目は、1つの事柄がいくつかの結果を生む形

   Civil wars have continued for five years in this region.

   ↓   ↓   ↓

   Effect 1   Effect 2   Effect 3
   No workforce No education No infrastructure

B) Organizations

Introduction: General to specific (news, example, history, definition, etc.)

Thesis statement: Some African countries suffer from poverty because of the
following reasons.

The first reason is civil wars.

The second reason is drought.

The third reason is diseases.

Restatement: Thus, the three reasons above cause severe poverty in some African
countries.
Brief summary
Final statement

Exercise: 2つの文が原因（cause）なのか結果（effect）なのか（　　　）に入れましょう。

1. (　　　　) Development of African nations started late.
   (　　　　) Most African countries were colonized.
2. (　　　　) Many people fled their countries because of civil war.
   (　　　　) People didn't have stable jobs.

II　Content

国際的な開発、貧困、飢餓、について、その定義や原因・結果について基本的な事柄を学習します。

A　Topic Introduction: **International development**

Read the passage and answer the questions that follow. Share and check your answers with your team. Use the 'Language for Learning' expressions (see page 6).

1

Disc2-13
45))

　　　In the field of international relations, the definition of development is crucial when we compare countries. One way of comparing countries is to measure their gross national income (GNI) per capita. Countries with high levels of GNI per capita are often referred to as developed countries, industrialized economies, or
5　members of the Global North. In contrast, common terms for countries with lower levels of GNI are developing countries, members of the Global South, and least developed countries (LDC). Yet, can we simply claim that a country is developed when it has a widening wealth gap between a rich minority and the poor majority? Similarly, can we say a country is developing when there is political oppression and
10　other human rights abuses? Although economic growth is a crucial factor, we now recognize that development means far more.

Question 1: Why is GNI not an adequate measure of a country's development?
Question 2: Internet Search ⊙ What is the trend in Japan's GNI? Compare it to one or two other countries?

> **Key terms**
>
> development 開発　　gross national income (GNI) per capita 一人あたりの国民総所得
> industrialized economies 工業経済、工業化途上経済　　the Global North 北の先進国
> developing countries 発展途上国　　the Global South 南の発展途上国　　least developed
> countries (LDC) 後発開発途上国　　a widening wealth gap 貧富の差の拡大　　political
> oppression 政治的抑圧、政治弾圧　　human rights abuses 人権侵害

A broader definition of development can refer to countries improving not only their economies, but also living standards, sustainability, equalities and freedoms. First published in 1990, the United Nations Development Programme (UNDP) Human Development Index (HDI) is a widely used measurement that
5 compares the development and progress of 189 countries. The HDI ranks each country's development based on three areas: standard of living, healthy life expectancy, and educational opportunity. The UN Human Development Report Office (HDRO) conducts further research in areas such as inequalities, human security, empowerment, and poverty. Through its extensive work in human
10 development, the UN aims to enrich the overall quality of human life by informing and challenging government policies.

Question 3: What measurement of development is used in 189 countries? What does it measure?

Question 4: Internet Search ▶ What is Japan's current HDI ranking and score? Do you think it is an adequate measurement of the development of Japan? Explain.

Key terms

a broader definition より広い意味、定義　sustainability 継続可能性　the United Nations Development Programme (UNDP) 国連開発計画　Human Development Index (HDI) 人間開発指数　UN Human Development Report Office (HDRO) 国連人間開発報告書事務局　human security 人間の安全保障　empowerment 社会・政治・経済権限などの付与

However we measure development, the world continues to be a very unequal place for millions of people. From a humanitarian perspective, we have a collective responsibility to improve this situation. Yet, there are other very important reasons why we must be concerned about international development. In 2021, there were
5 46 countries on the United Nations' list of least developed countries (LDCs), most being in Africa, South America, and Asia/Oceania. Typically, LDCs have high levels of poverty, lack strong institutions, for example education and justice, and have weak governance. Such conditions can lead to instability, conflict, and terrorism, which can spread internationally. Thus, development assistance for countries in
10 these regions has the potential to create a more stable and secure international society for all.

Question 5: Why is international development important?

Question 6: Internet Search ▶ JICA (Japan International Cooperation Agency) provides development assistance to many countries worldwide. Go to the JICA website→ jica.go.jp → 「各国における取り組み」and read about a country of your choice. Then present what you learnt to your team.

To learn about the LDCs that JICA supports, compare JICA's list of countries [https://www.jica.go.jp/regions/index.html] with the UN's list of LDCs [https://unctad.org/topic/least-developed-countries/list].

Key terms

humanitarian 人道主義の、人道主義的な　　**a collective responsibility** 集団責任　**Asia/Oceania** アジア・オセアニア地域　　**strong institutions** 教育制度・司法機関などの持続可能な国家機関　　**justice** 正義　　**weak governance** 貧弱な統治　　**development assistance** 開発援助

B **Three-Step Discussion**

First, prepare your ideas about the topic in Japanese. Share and develop your ideas with your home team and then write out an opinion in English. Make new groups and share/discuss your ideas in English. Be sure to use your 'Language for Learning' and 'Discussion Phrases' (see page 6).

Discussion Question: Do you think it is important for Japan to provide development assistance to countries in Africa, or should Japan focus more on Asia/Oceania? Explain.

Example response: "Personally, I think that Japan spends too much on development assistance to other countries, whatever the region. Japan is prone to natural disasters and has its own poverty issues. We should be focusing more on Japan's problems and find other ways to assist foreign countries."

III **Writing Task: Research and write about causes and effects of poverty.**

日本、またはある国の貧困の原因を調べ、実施されている解決策があればそれも含めて説明してみましょう。
まず、次の英文構造を確認します。

Poverty in Niger

The Republic of the Niger is located in West Africa and two-thirds of its land is in the Sahara Desert. It is a hot, <u>landlocked</u> country sharing borders with seven countries, namely Mali, Algeria, Libya, Chad, Nigeria, Benin, and Burkina Faso. Since it became independent from France in 1960, the economy has <u>stagnated</u>
5 many times. In 2018, the International Monetary Fund (IMF) ranked Niger 11th among the 28 poorest countries, and <u>GDP per capita</u> was $510 (Martin, 2018). There are three major reasons for the poverty in Niger: a high birth rate, seasonal <u>droughts</u>, and an unstable government.

The first reason is a high birth rate. The World Data Atlas reports that the birth
10 rate in 2020 was 6.7 births per woman, and the rate of increase was 3.8 % (Knoema, 2020). In 2022, the population of Niger was about 26 million, and it was predicted that the country might have a <u>population explosion</u>. With this growing population, it was very difficult to support and educate families. In fact, Niger's <u>literacy rate</u> is improving, but still one of the worst in the world. On average, the literacy rate of
15 Nigeriens aged 15 to 24 was only 39.7% (Giovetti, 2019). As a result, with few skills and little education, people cannot break the <u>vicious circle</u> of poverty.

The second reason is seasonal droughts. These droughts accelerate <u>desertification</u> and <u>devastate</u> farmland, which makes up only 10% of the country. This leads to a shortage of both food and drinking water, causing <u>malnutrition</u> and
20 the spread of diseases such as cholera. It is difficult to solve this problem because water storage and transport systems, such as dams and water pipes, have become very old or were never constructed. Most dams in Niger were built in the 1960s and 1970s, and the government is short of money for improvements (Hitachi, n.d.). Another negative effect of these droughts is that they create conflicts with locals,
25 when people move to find new land to farm.

The third reason for poverty in Niger is an unstable government. Food shortages create a wide gap between the rich and poor, which <u>upsets</u> the stability of the government. The Nigerian government was <u>overthrown</u> by <u>military coups</u> at least four times between 1974 and 2010. In addition, the spread of poverty
30 allows terrorist activities such as the Islamic group Boko Haram. In 2015, when the Nigerian government fought with Boko Haram, over 115,000 people were <u>displaced</u> and became refugees (The Borgen Project, 2017). These types of incidents have <u>disrupted</u> the economic development of Niger.

In conclusion, poverty in Niger is caused by three major reasons; a high
35 birth rate, seasonal droughts, and an unstable government. Many people in other countries are now aware that these are not only Niger's problems, but global

problems because they affect other countries in many ways. Led by the UN, some NGOs and business corporations have started to provide help to Niger. Hopefully the situation will gradually improve.

References

Giovetti, O. (2019, September 26). *Education in Niger: When enrollment is high, but literacy is low.* Retrieved March 22, 2022 from https://www.concernusa.org/story/education-in-niger/

Hitachi. (n.d.). *Global Innovation Report. Kanbatsuga afurickatairikuni ataerueikyou [The influence of drought on Africa].* Retrieved March 23, 2022 from https://www.hitachihyoron.com/jp/archive/2010s/2017/04/Global_Innovation/index.html?WT.mc_id=ksearch

Knoema. (2020). Nigeeru jinkouzouka [Population increase in Niger]. In ワールド・データ・アトラス *[World Data Atlas].* Retrieved March 22 from https://jp.knoema.com/atlas/%E3%83%8B%E3%82%B8%E3%82%A7%E3%83%BC%E3%83%AB/%E4%BA%BA%E5%8F%A3%E5%A2%97%E5%8A%A0

Martin, W. (2018, July 3). Sekaide mottomo mazushiikuni waasuto 28 [The poorest country among the 28 poorest countries]. Retrieved March 20, 2022 from https://www.businessinsider.jp/post-168683

TBS NEWS. (2019, July 15). *Nishiafurika・Nigeeru no genjyou [Current situation of Niger in West Africa].* Retrieved March 24, 2022 from https://www.youtube.com/watch?v=Y6zoZiaIKNA

The Borgen Project. (2017, September 13). *Causes of poverty in Niger.* Retrieved March 24, 2022 from https://borgenproject.org/causes-of-poverty-in-niger/

Key terms

landlocked 陸地で囲まれた　　stagnated よどむ、沈滞する　　GDP per capita 一人あたりのGDP　droughts 日照り　　population explosion 人口爆発　　literacy rate 識字率　　vicious circle 悪循環　　desertification 砂漠化　　devastate 荒廃させる　　malnutrition 栄養不良　　upset だめにする　　overthrown 倒された　　military coup 軍事クーデター　　displaced 故郷から移動させられた　　disrupted 混乱させる、中断させる

Question 1: The thesis statement に波線を引きましょう。

Question 2: 3つの理由（原因）のフレーズを四角で囲みましょう。

Question 3: このエッセイの因果関係が分かる図を描きましょう。

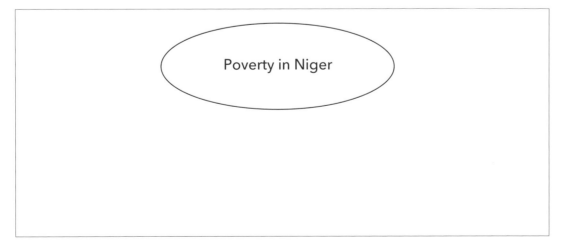

貧困に苦しんでいる国を1つ選び、その原因について5パラグラフのエッセイを書きましょう。
1パラグラフ100 wordsをめざして書いてみましょう。

Topic:
Thesis statement:

Outline:

Ⅳ　Grammar for Writing

A) 原因と結果の表現

1. since
   because
   due to
   thanks to
   owing to
   as a result of
   as a consequence of, consequently,
   therefore,
   because of
   thus, hence,

2. affect
   cause
   result from
   result in
   be responsible for
   lead to

Exercise　（→p. 128参照）

The climate crisis

Can Do

Structure: 原因と結果のエッセイの構成を知る。
Content: 世界の気候変動について知り、説明できる。

S: 原因と結果についてのエッセイを書けるようにします。
C: 世界の気候変動について基本的な事柄、問題について学習し、説明できるようにします。

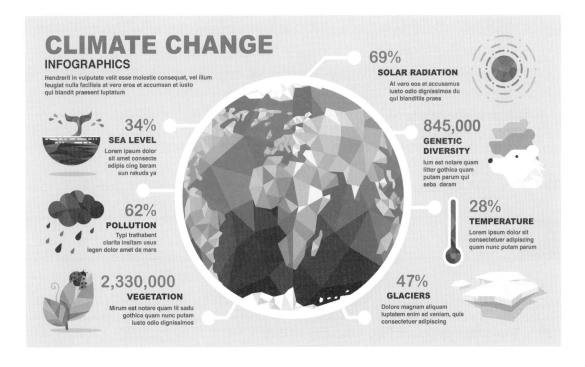

I Cause and Effect (See Unit 11)

A) 原因と結果のエッセイには、大きく分けて２つの形があります。

1. The cause essay: 1つの結果 ← いくつかの原因
   Bodyの部分で、原因を書く。
2. The effect essay: 1つの原因 → いくつかの結果
   Bodyの部分で結果を書く。
(3. The cause chain essay: 原因と結果が連鎖する。これは、通常1の形でも2の形でも起こりうる)

B) Organizations

Introduction: news, example, history, definition, etc.

Thesis statement: There are several negative effects of deforestation.

The first effect is ～ .

The second effect is ～ .

The third effect is ～ .

In conclusion, deforestation causes three major negative effects ～ .

Concluding statement

ここで使えるつなぎ言葉

Therefore,　As a result,　As a consequence,　Consequently,　For this reason

II　Content

気候変動についての基本的な事柄を学習します。

A　Topic Introduction: **The climate crisis**

✎ What do you know about global warming and climate change issues? First, make some notes below, and then share your ideas with a partner or your team.

- _____
- _____
- _____

Next, working in teams of three, each student will read one of the paragraphs below by themselves and make notes, summarizing the key points.

1

　　The UN defines *climate change* as long-term changes in global temperatures and weather patterns. Previously, there had been periods of natural climate change, but since the Industrial Revolution in the 1800s, human activity has been the main cause of a rapid rise in global temperatures and extreme weather. Rising
5　temperatures are causing irreversible environmental damage, rising sea levels, natural disasters, economic disruption, conflict, increased poverty, and even terrorism in regions most vulnerable to climate change. The situation is now so urgent that many scientists and politicians are using the terms *climate crisis* and *climate emergency* to talk about climate change.

Key terms

climate change 気候変動　　the Industrial Revolution 産業革命　　extreme weather 異常気象
irreversible 不可逆的　　disruption 混乱　　vulnerable ～の悪影響に受けやすい

2

　　The rise in global temperatures is mainly caused by greenhouse gas emissions, which are like a blanket wrapped around the earth, trapping the sun's heat and raising temperatures. Carbon dioxide (CO_2) emissions cause the most damage. CO_2 comes mainly from burning fossil fuels (e.g., coal, oil, and gas) to provide
5　energy for transport, manufacturing, electricity, and heating. It is also produced by deforestation and other industrial processes, such as making cement and steel. Another major emission comes from methane. Human activity produces about 60% of this through agriculture (e.g., cattle and deforestation) and the energy sector (International Energy Agency, 2020). We are now producing greenhouse gas
10　emissions at a record high, and show no signs of slowing down.

Key terms

greenhouse gas emissions 温室効果ガスの排出　　carbon dioxide (CO_2) 二酸化炭素
burning fossil fuels 化石燃料燃焼　　coal, oil, and gas 石炭、石油、ガス　　deforestation 森林伐採　　industrial processes 産業プロセス、工業工程　　methane メタン（ガス）　　agriculture 農業
the energy sector エネルギー産業

The majority of greenhouse gas emissions are produced by highly populated, industrialized economies, namely China, the United States, India, Russia, and Japan. With the exception of India, these countries are also major producers of emissions per capita. The majority of developing countries produce only small
5   emissions, yet they are the most vulnerable to climate change. In 2015, the Paris Agreement, an international treaty on climate change, was created. To date, 191 UN member states have signed this treaty, which aims to limit global warming to 2°C, ideally 1.5°C, by the year 2100. However, despite their promises, many countries are still far from the rate of progress we need to achieve these ambitious targets.
10 As the environmental, humanitarian, economic, and social costs of climate change are close to irreversible, the time for action is right now. In the words of António Guterres, Secretary-General of the United Nations, "We are in a race against the clock and no one is safe from the destructive effects of climate disruption" (UN, 2021).

Key terms

industrialized economies 工業経済、工業化途上経済　　per capita 一人当たり　　the Paris Agreement パリ協定　　an international treaty 国際条約　　the rate of progress 進行速度
Secretary-General of the United Nations 国際連合事務総長

References

International Energy Agency. (2020, March). *Methane Tracker*. Retrieved February 26, 2022 from https://www.iea.org/reports/methane-tracker-2020

UN. (2021, December 9). *People, countries impacted by climate change also vulnerable to terrorist recruitment, violence, speakers tell Security Council in open debate*. Retrieved February 26, 2022 from https://www.un.org/press/en/2021/sc14728.doc.htm

B   Team Share: **Understanding the Climate Crisis**

Share your summaries and understanding with other students in your team. Listen and take notes carefully. Don't forget to use the 'Language for Learning' expressions (see page 6)!

C   **Topic Reflection**

Internet Search ▶ What do you still want to know about the climate crisis? Ask your team members and then do a brief internet search.

D **Four-Step Discussion**

By yourself, prepare two or three ideas in Japanese. Then share and develop your ideas with your home team. You might be able to add more details or make more concrete suggestions. Next, by yourself write out one or more of your ideas in English and get ready to share it with a new team. Be sure to use your 'Language for Learning' and 'Discussion Phrases' (see page 6).

What can you personally do to fight the climate emergency? Think of two or three concrete ideas, providing reasons and details to support your suggestions.

● _____

_____

● _____

_____

● _____

_____

Your Final Idea:

III	**Writing Task:**	Research and write about causes and effects on a topic of your choice.

世界の気候変動について、問題を1つ選び、その原因と結果を書きます。Unit 11 で原因を扱ったので、この Unit 12 では、結果を扱います。
まず、次の英文構造を確認します。

The Destruction of Forests

Disc2-20
52 »)

Forests around the world have been disappearing rapidly. From 2019 to 2020, for example, huge fires in Australia burned many trees as well as koalas and kangaroos. These fires are believed to have been ignited by natural heat and burned as much land as half the area of Japan. People also cut down trees to burn
5 as fuel, make houses, and create farms for "slash-and-burn" agriculture. There are several major negative effects of deforestation, including global warming, floods and landslides, and it has an impact on people's everyday lives.

The first effect is global warming. Trees absorb CO_2 and produce oxygen. If the number of trees is reduced and the amount of CO_2 increases, heat will not
10 be released from the earth, and temperatures will rise, like in a greenhouse. This causes ice in Antarctica to melt and sea levels to rise, which means many islands will be submerged. It also accelerates desertification and destroys farmlands. Because of this, the fires of the Amazon Rainforest are of great concern because this forest is said to create 20% of the Earth's oxygen (Life Manual, 2020).

15 The second effect is that deforestation increases the possibility of floods and landslides. Trees are often cut down to make room for farmland, tourist resorts, and water-power generators. If you think of a mountain with no trees, you can imagine the catastrophes that heavy rains could cause. For example, in May of 2021, a tropical cyclone hit India and Bangladesh, and about 1.2 million were
20 evacuated with a damage of 3 billion dollars. In July, heavy rains in China caused extreme flooding and claimed 302 people with a damage of $17.6 billion. In August, hurricane Ida hit Louisiana in the US and claimed 95 people with a damage of $65 billion (Yi, 2021).

The third effect is that deforestation has a direct impact on people's everyday
25 lives. The loss of forests increases temperatures, along with infectious diseases such as malaria, which is carried by mosquitoes. Furthermore, the availability of forest products, such as edible mushrooms, fruits, and plants decreases. Additionally, conflicts over the ownership of forests have occurred because of developing countries which experience population explosions, creating a higher demand for
30 wood and paper products. Shortages of these products create conflicts between foreign companies and local peoples (Gurilabo, 2022).

In conclusion, deforestation causes three major negative effects; global warming, floods and landslides, and it has an impact on people's everyday lives. These are problems that many people around the world have experienced. Now
35 more than ever, it is important to understand that forests are an essential part of our world and must be protected.

References

Gurilabo (2022, April 7). *Shinrinhakaino chikyuuheno eikyoutoha? [What is the impact of deforestation?]*. Retrieved June 18, 2022 from https://gurilabo.igrid.co.jp/article/2410/

Life Manual. (2020). *Nihontosekaiga kakaeru Kannkyoumondai 25 [25 environmental problems in Japan and the world]*. Retrieved March 29, 2022 from https://22nd-century.jp/environment-issues/solutions/#toc1

Yi. (2021, December 30). *Anguru: 2021nen, kikouhenndouniyoru ijoukishouga motarashita higaiha [Angle: How much damage was caused by extreme weather due to climate change]*. Reuters. Retrieved March 29, 2022 from https://jp.reuters.com/article/global-climate-disasters-idJPKBN2J70K6

Key terms

ignited 着火される　　slash-and-burn agriculture 焼き畑農業　deforestation 森林伐採
absorb 吸収する　　oxygen 酸素　　Antarctica 南極　　submerged 水中に沈んだ　accelerate
促進する　rainforest 熱帯雨林　　water-power generators 水力発電機　a tropical cyclone
熱帯低気圧　evacuated 避難させられる　　claim 犠牲者を出す　　infectious diseases 伝染病
edible 食用に適する　population explosions 人口爆発　　conflicts 闘争、争い

Question 1: The thesis statement に波線を引きましょう。

Question 2: 3つの「森林伐採」がもたらす結果の文を四角で囲みましょう。

Question 3: このエッセイの因果関係が分かる図を描きましょう。

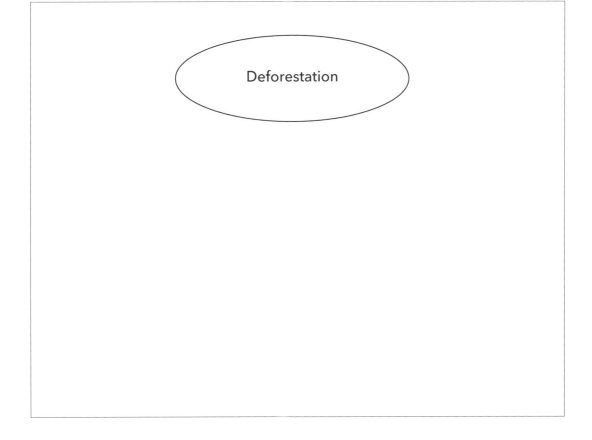

Your Writing

気候変動の問題点について1つトピックを選び、5 パラグラフのエッセイを書きましょう。1
パラグラフ100 wordsをめざして書いてみましょう。

Topic:
Thesis statement:

Outline:

Ⅳ　Grammar for Writing

A. 結果を述べるつなぎ言葉

　　accordingly
　　as a consequence
　　as it turned out
　　consequently
　　for that reason
　　thus
　　hence
　　therefore
　　inevitably
　　necessarily
　　that being the case

Exercise　（→p. 129参照）

Unit 13　Global trade

Can Do

Structure: 問題と解決のエッセイの構成を知る。
Content: 世界的な貿易機構、自由貿易と保護貿易について知る。

S: 問題と解決について
　 のエッセイを書ける
　 ようにします。

C: 基本的な世界貿易機
　 構について学習し、
　 自由貿易と保護貿易
　 について、説明できるようにします。

Ⅰ　Problem and Solution

A) 問題と解決のエッセイには、大きく分けて２つの形があります。

1. 問題とその原因を書き、少しだけ解決策に触れる。—Type 1
　 問題を提示することが目的になる。

2. 問題と解決策を書く。主に、その解決策の効果、実行可能性、他の解決策よりよいことな
　 どを書く。

　 A. 解決策を提示することが目的になる。構成に２つのパターンがある。—Type 2-A-1/
　 　 A-2

　 B. 上のAの書き方プラス、それに反対論を入れて、その反対論にさらに反論する書き方
　 　 もある。—Type 2-B

B) Organizations

Type 1: 問題を提示するエッセイ

Introduction: (news, example, history, definition, etc.) Thesis statement: 問題がある
The first problem is ～ . （原因や例）
The second problem is ～ .
The third problem is ～ .
In conclusion, restatement of the thesis statement Concluding sentences

Type 2-A-1: Bodyの部分で3つ（2つ）の解決策を提示するエッセイ

Introduction: (news, example, history, definition, etc.) (問題の説明や重要性) Thesis statement: 解決策がある
The first solution is ～. (この解決策の実行性・有効性・例など)
The second solution is ～. (この解決策の実行性・有効性・例など)
The third solution is ～. （この解決策の実行性・有効性・例など）
In conclusion, restatement of the thesis statement Concluding sentences

Type 2-A-2: Bodyの第2パラグラフで問題と原因、Bodyの第3パラグラフでその原因への解決策を書く。

Introduction: (news, example, history, definition, etc.) Thesis statement:
Problem and causes
Solutions
In conclusion, restatement of the thesis statement Concluding sentences

Type 2-B: 解決策を提示するエッセイ＋反論＋その反論

Introduction: (news, example, history, definition, etc.) (問題の説明や重要性) Thesis statement: 解決策がある
The first solution is ～. (この解決策の実行性・有効性・例など)
The second solution is ～. (この解決策の実行性・有効性・例など)
上のような解決策ではだめだという、自分の意見とは反対の人の意見 　　↑ その反論への反論を書く
In conclusion, restatement of the thesis statement Concluding sentences

II　Content

世界の貿易機構、自由貿易、保護貿易について学習します。

A　Topic Introduction: **Global trade**

Read the passage and answer the questions that follow. Share and check your answers with your team. Use the 'Language for Learning' expressions (see page 6).

1

Disc2-21
53))

After the Second World War, international society aimed to overcome problems arising from protectionism, which had increased since 1871, and trade restrictions that were imposed between World Wars I and II. This collective effort led to the General Agreement on Trade and Tariffs (GATT) in 1947, which was later superseded by the World Trade Organization (WTO) in 1995. Currently, the WTO has 164 members, accounting for 98% of total world trade, with 22 other countries negotiating membership. The WTO encompasses all goods, services, and intellectual property, as well as some investment policies. The WTO's main objective is to help trade flow freely, smoothly, and predictably. It aims to achieve this by:

- administering trade agreements;
- providing a forum for trade negotiations;
- settling trade disputes;
- reviewing national trade policies;
- building the trade of developing economies; and
- cooperating with other international organizations.

Question 1: Which organization preceded the WTO?

Question 2: What is the main objective of the WTO?

Question 3: Internet Search ▶ When did Japan join the WTO?

Key terms

protectionism 保護貿易主義　trade restrictions 貿易制限　General Agreement on Trade and Tariffs (GATT) 関税及び貿易に関する一般協定　superseded 取って代わられた　World Trade Organization (WTO) 世界貿易機関　intellectual property 知的財産権　investment policies 投資政策　administering trade agreements 貿易協定を管理する　providing a forum for ～できる公開討論の場を提供する　trade disputes 通商摩擦、争議行為

---

2 (Disc2-22) 54

　　Through free trade, the WTO aims to provide assurance for consumers, producers, and exporters. For instance, by removing tariffs on imports, consumers can enjoy a cheaper and wider choice of products and services. By diversifying supply chains, producers can establish a more stable supply of the raw materials they need for manufacturing. With agreed rules on trade, exporters know that global markets will remain open to them. By lowering trade barriers through negotiations among member governments, the WTO's system also breaks down other barriers between countries and their peoples. This has the potential for a more stable and peaceful world. The WTO also aims to settle trade frictions between countries before disputes spill over into economic, political or military conflict. In the WTO, decisions are normally made by consensus among all members.

Question 4: In what ways does free trade benefit consumers, producers, and exporters?

Question 5: How might the WTO contribute to maintaining peace in international society?

Question 6: [Internet Search ▶] Find an example of a recent trade dispute which the WTO helped to settle. Explain it to a partner or your team.

Key terms

free trade 自由貿易　　consumers, producers, and exporters 消費者、製造者、輸出［業］者　removing tariffs 関税の撤廃　　diversifying supply chains 供給網を多様化する　　raw materials 原材料、原料　　global markets 世界市場　　lowering trade barriers 貿易障壁を下げる　　break down other barriers 他の垣根を取り払う、障壁を取り除く　　peoples 複数の民族　　trade frictions 貿易摩擦　　spill over into に波及する　decisions ~ made by consensus 総意による決定

3

Disc2-23
55))

　　　Critics of free trade, including many <u>opponents of</u> economic globalization, raise concerns that it is not always in everyone's best interests. They point out that in developing economies it can lead to environmental damage, <u>unethical business practices</u>, and <u>the exploitation of natural resources and workers</u>. For instance, most
5　developed economies have strict <u>labor laws</u> regarding working hours and time off, wages, safety, healthcare, and so on. The <u>drawback</u> for companies operating there is the cost of producing goods and services can increase as a result. Many developing countries, in contrast, offer far less legal protection, especially to <u>low-skilled workers</u>. By <u>outsourcing</u> production, customer support, and other business-
10　related tasks there, foreign companies are able to <u>reduce overheads</u> and operate at a far lower cost. While outsourcing increases profits and provides work for the local population, it can <u>perpetuate</u> the exploitation of workers, not to mention <u>the hollowing out of industries</u> and unemployment in the company's home country.

Question 7: What criticisms have been made against free trade?

Question 8: In developing countries, how might low-skilled workers be exploited?

Question 9: [Internet Search ▶] Which country is the largest outsourcer? What are the top five destinations for outsourcing? What are the most outsourced jobs globally?

Key terms

opponents of ～の反対者　　unethical business practices 非倫理的行為、不公正な取引方法　the exploitation of natural resources and local workers 天然資源の開発と現地労働者の搾取　labor laws 労働法　　drawback 欠点　　low-skilled workers 未熟練労働者　　outsourcing 業務を海外への外注　　reduce overheads 間接費を削減する　　perpetuate 永続させる　the hollowing out of industries 産業の空洞化

B) Team Quiz

Make teams of three. Take turns to ask each other a question in the order, 1 to 9. Don't forget to use the 'Language for Learning' expressions (see page 6).

Student 1

Q1: The General Agreement on Trade and Tariffs (GATT) was established to avoid problems arising from protectionism and trade restrictions. True or False?

Q4: With free trade, the World Trade Organization (WTO) aims to ensure greater choice, securer supplies, open markets, and so on. True or False?

Q7: Critics of free trade are concerned about environmental damage, unethical business practices, and the exploitation of natural resources and workers? True or False?

Student 2

Q2: The World Trade Organization (WTO) replaced the GATT, which currently has 164 members and represents 96% of world trade. True or False?

Q5: The WTO aims to lower cultural and trade barriers through negotiations among member governments. True or False?

Q8: The lack of strict labor laws in many developing countries can be beneficial to foreign companies. True or False?

Student 3

Q3: If members disagree over trade, the World Trade Organization (WTO) can help to settle the dispute. True or False?

Q6: Members cannot oppose decisions made in the WTO. True or False?

Q9: Outsourcing has a negative effect on industries in the home country. True or False?

C) Three-Step Discussion

First, prepare your ideas about the topic in Japanese. Share and develop your ideas with your home team and then write out an opinion in English. Make new groups and share/discuss your ideas in English. Be sure to use your 'Language for Learning' and 'Discussion Phrases' (see page 6).

Discussion Question: Do you think free trade between countries helps to prevent economic, political or military conflict? Explain.

Example response: "In principle, yes, free trade is supposed to help avoid conflict. However, former US President Donald Trump complained that the US was importing too much from China, which was damaging to American industries. Whether or not his complaint was justified, he started an economic trade-war that led to higher costs for manufacturers, higher prices for consumers, and increased political tensions with China."

	Writing Task:	Research and write about problems and solutions of the trade between two countries of your choice

世界の貿易問題について、2つの国、または地域を選び、その問題と解決策（またはどちらか）を書きます。まず、次の英文構造を確認します。

Trade Issues Between Japan and the US

　　After WWII, the US did not allow Japan to rebuild <u>industrial facilities</u> to help recover their economic power. However, as the US-Soviet conflict deepened and <u>the People's Republic of China</u> was founded, the US decided to use Japan's strategic location in their fight against <u>communism</u>. The Korean War helped <u>boost</u>
5 Japan's economy, which fully recovered during the 1960s. Despite this, US-Japan trade frictions continued until recently, affected throughout time by political situations and events happening around the world (Warashibekawaraban, 2020). Even after 2020, when the Japan-US <u>Trade Agreement</u> concluded, two major trade issues remained between Japan and the US.

10 　　The first issue was automobiles, an industry that was very important for both countries. From around 2017, 1.7 million cars were exported annually to the US from Japan. During this same time, however, only about 100,000 cars were imported from the US to Japan. This <u>imbalance</u> of exports and imports became a concern for the US because 80% of the US <u>trade deficit</u> was caused by automobiles.
15 To protect US car companies such as General Motors, Ford, and Chrysler, the US <u>imposed customs duties</u> for <u>passenger cars</u> and car parts at 2.5%, and trucks at 25%. On the other hand, Japan did not impose any <u>tariffs</u> on American automobiles, and demanded that the US reduce them for automobiles from Japan. In the bilateral agreement, as well as in the <u>Trans-Pacific-Partnership (TPP)</u>, former President
20 Obama promised to <u>eliminate</u> tariffs for Japan on passenger cars at 2.5%, but with a 25-year <u>grace period</u> and 30 years for trucks. Moreover, former President Trump abruptly removed the US from the TPP, and demanded that the market be opened, instead of raising tariffs to 25% (Nikkei, 2019). As a result, with fear that the US might set additional tariffs and limit the quota of imports, Japan agreed to 2.5%
25 tariffs for passenger cars. Thus, even as recently as November 2021, negotiations had ceased (Asahi Shimbun Digital, 2021).

　　The second issue was agricultural products. Both Japan and the US had special reasons to protect their farmers and agricultural industries. In the US, midwestern agricultural states such as Nebraska and Wisconsin were important
30 for <u>the presidential election</u>. In Japan, maintaining <u>the food self-sufficiency rate</u> was crucial. Furthermore, after the US left the TPP, they had to compete

with EU and TPP members in the Japanese market. In the 2020 Japan-US Trade Agreement, Japan was able to protect their native rice industry, but tariffs on other agricultural products were set to 37%. However, 38.5% tariffs on beef were supposed
35 to reduce gradually to 9%. For this, Japanese consumers were able to buy US beef inexpensively, but Japan was at a disadvantage for production costs because the US used large-scale farming systems. Therefore, Japan took measures to reduce production costs, increase product quality, and provide subsidies to small and medium-sized livestock farmers (Kakuya, 2020).

40   In conclusion, there were two major issues in trade between Japan and the US. The first was automobiles and the second was agricultural products. To solve these trade issues, both governments had to take multiple measures to support their industries domestically, as well as engaging in tough negotiations internationally. All of this had to be done while following the rules of the WTO for enjoying the
45 benefits of free trade.

Key terms

industrial facilities 工業施設   the People's Republic of China 中華人民共和国
communism 共産主義   boost 押し上げる   trade agreement 貿易協定   imbalance 不均衡
trade deficit 貿易赤字   impose customs duties 関税を課す   passenger cars 乗用車
tariffs 関税   Trans-Pacific-Partnership (TPP) 環太平洋パートナーシップ協定   eliminate 取り
はらう、なくす   grace period 猶予期間   the presidential election 大統領選挙   the food
self-sufficiency rate 食糧自給率   large-scale farming systems 大規模農場システム
subsidies 助成金   medium-sized livestock farmers 中小規模農場

Question 1: The thesis statement に下線を引きましょう。

Question 2: 日米の貿易問題と、その解決策を表に書きましょう。（→ p. 130参照）

References

Asahi Shimbun Digital. (2021, November 25). Beijidoushakannzei `teppai zentei' no tōben mamore [Defending the explanation about the US automobile tariff "premise of abolition"]. *Asahi Shimbun.* Retrieved March 27, 2022 from https://www.asahi.com/articles/DA3S15122128.html

Kakuya, S. (2020, February 14). *Tsuini hakkousareta nichibeibouekikyoutei, nihonnnonougyou・nousannbutsueno eikyouwa? [The Japan-US Trade Agreement reached. Did it affect agriculture and agricultural products in Japan?].* Retrieved March 21, 2022 from https://smartagri-jp.com/agriculture/1151

Nikkei. (2019, September 26). *Jidoushazeitoha-nihonga yunyusuru beikokuseiniha kakarazu [What are the automobile tariffs-No Tariffs on the American cars to Japan].* Retrieved March 27, 2022 from https://www.nikkei.com/article/DGXMZO50251000W9A920C1EA2000/

Warashibekawaraban. (2020, December 25). *Imadakarakikeru nishibeibouekimasatsunoshinsou-rekishiohimotohi honshitsutekigenino saguru [Deep reasons currently found for the Japan-US trade friction].* Retrieved March 10, 2022 from http://www.am-one.co.jp/warashibe/article/chiehako-20201225-1.html

世界の貿易問題からトピックを選び、問題点と解決策を4つか5つのパラグラフで書きましょう。エッセイの構成は前のページを見て決めましょう（トピックの例：US-China, EU, EU-UK, etc.）。

IV Grammar for Writing

A. Problem and Solution の表現

1. problems を表す言葉
   issues, concerns, worries
2. solutions を表す言葉
   measures, suggestions,

   can be solved
   take measures
   solve the problem
   solutions to problems (solutions to the problem)

B. 英語のcollocation：単語と単語のよく使われる組み合わせを指す。日本語では、連結語句、連語と言われる。

日米貿易のエッセイの中で出てきたもの

1. The Japan-US Trade Agreement <u>concluded</u> in 2020.
                      was signed
                      was reached
   The Japan and the US <u>came to</u> an agreement.
                  reached
                  arrived at

2. The US <u>imposed customs duties for</u> passenger cars at 2.5%.
       imposed tariffs
       imposed taxes on the company

3. ～ because the US <u>adopted</u> large-scale farming <u>systems</u> ～
                employed
                used

4. ～ , both governments were required to <u>take</u> multiple <u>measures to</u> ～
                              take   measures against ～
                          come up with measures

5. ～ while following the rules of the WTO for <u>enjoying</u> the <u>benefits</u> of free trade.
                          experiencing the benefits
                          receiving the benefits

Exercise （→p. 131参照）

Unit 14 Considering global issues from both sides

Can Do

Structure: 説得力のあるエッセイの構成を知る。
Content: あるトピックに関して両面の意見を知る。

S: 説得力のあるエッセイを書けるようにします。
C: あるトピックについて両サイドの意見を知り、説明できるようにします。

I Argumentative Essay

A) 目的：

自分の意見や立場を説明して、意見や立場の違う人を説得することです。そのためには、論理的で、かつエビデンスや例などで、自分の意見が正しいことを証明できることが必要です。

B) トピック：

国際政治の分野では、次のようなものが、トピックになります。

Exercise： 2番のところに、反対意見のthesis statementを書きましょう。

1. Nuclear energy should be used.
2.

1. Countries should ban tariffs and promote free trade.
2.

1. Immigrants should be allowed to enter any country with no conditions.
2.

C) Organization

1.

Introduction (news, examples, history, definition, etc.)

Thesis statement: should/should not

The first reason is ～ . (examples, evidence, statistics, etc.)

The second reason is ～ . (examples, evidence, statistics, etc.)

The third reason is ～ . (examples, evidence, statistics, etc.)

In conclusion, restatement of the thesis statement

Concluding sentences

2.

Introduction (news, examples, history, definition, etc.)

Thesis statement: should/should not

The first reason is ～ . (examples, evidence, statistics, etc.)

The second reason is ～ . (examples, evidence, statistics, etc.)

There are some people who disagree with ～ because ～ . (自分とは反対の意見を載せる) However, it is not true because ～ . (それに対して、自分の反論をする)

（英語で "refute"、日本語で「反駁する」と言う。ここで、大事なのは、上の2つの理由とかぶらないこと）

In conclusion, restatement of the thesis statement.

Concluding sentences

II　Content

ここでは、日本の憲法9条の改正についての議論を読みます。ライティングの見本も兼ねているので、内容と形、両方とも注意して見てください。

1

Disc2-25
57))

　　　The Japanese Constitution was created after World War II, becoming law on May 3 1947. Article 9 of the constitution states that Japan will not maintain a military and may only go to war in order to defend itself from an attack. However, in 2015 the Liberal Democratic Party (LDP) created new laws which allow Japan
5 to defend its allies in international combat (i.e., *collective self-defense*). Furthermore, the LDP aims to revise the constitution in order to recognize its military and make greater use of it internationally. There are objections to these changes, however I support revising Article 9 of the constitution.

> **Key terms**
>
> Japanese Constitution 日本国憲法　　Article 9 第9条　　the Liberal Democratic Party (LDP) 自由民主党　　collective self-defense 集団的自衛権　　revise the constitution 日本国憲法を改定する

2

Disc2-26
58))

　　　One reason is Article 9 does not reflect the current reality. Over the last 70 years, Japan has developed one of the world's most powerful militaries. Starting in 1950, Japan introduced the National Police Reserve, which consisted of 75,000 men who were trained in warfare. Then, in 1954, Prime Minister Yoshida established the
5 Japan Self-Defense Forces (JSDF), which had separate land, sea and air forces. Since then, the JSDF has grown and there are now approximately 250,000 active personnel. In terms of its military strength, in 2021, Japan ranked fifth globally, exceeded only by the US, Russia, China, and India (Global Firepower, 2022). In short, the constitution does not reflect the fact that Japan has one of the strongest
10 military forces in the world.

> **Key terms**
>
> National Police Reserve 警察予備隊　　warfare 戦争行為　　Japan Self-Defense Forces (JSDF) 自衛隊　　active personnel 軍事（兵士の）現役勤務

A further reason for revising Article 9 is the rapidly changing security situation in the Asia-Pacific. China has begun to make aggressive claims over territories in the East China Sea and South China Sea, challenging both international laws and Japan's sovereignty. Its warplanes, warships and other government vessels
5 are increasingly violating Japanese territory, especially near the Senkaku Islands. Russia is also increasing its military activity. In 2021, its warplanes violated Japanese airspace 258 times (Ministry of Defense, 2021). Russia has placed missile systems near disputed islands off the northern coast of Hokkaido and in March 2022 conducted missile tests in the area. In light of Russia's invasion of Ukraine in
10 February 2022, its behavior is a grave matter of concern for Japan. As security in the Asia-Pacific becomes increasingly severe, changing Article 9 of the constitution will strengthen Japan's alliances and position in the region.

> **Key terms**
>
> **East China Sea** 東シナ海　　**South China Sea** 南シナ海　　**government vessels** 官船、政府船
> **violating Japanese territory** 日本の領土を侵犯する　　**disputed islands** 北方領土問題・紛争の渦
> 中にある島　**conduct missile tests**（弾道）ミサイルなどのテストを行う　　**Russia's invasion of**
> **Ukraine** ロシアのウクライナ侵攻　　**a grave matter of concern** 重大問題

While the above arguments clearly support changing the constitution, there are also valid arguments against doing so. According to Nakano Koichi, a professor of politics at Sophia University, changing Japan's pacifist constitution risks "the destruction of the very foundation of our society" (BBC Online, 2015). Whereas
5 one viewpoint argues that Article 9 must change to reflect today's security realities, those in opposition claim that the government's policies must change to match Japan's pacifist constitution. Masaru Tamamoto, a prominent academic and international author, hoped that Japan, as a powerful and influential country, could "spread pacifism in the region to make this area ... a more stable and peaceful place"
10 (BBC Online, 2015). In his view, by changing the constitution, this opportunity would be lost. Furthermore, turning Japan into an active military force might lead to a regional security dilemma. In that case, paradoxically, Japan might end up less secure than before.

> **Key terms**
>
> **valid arguments** 妥当な議論　　**pacifist constitution** 平和主義の憲法　　**security dilemma** 安全
> 保障のジレンマ

5

In conclusion, while there are various opinions on the issue, I believe that changing Article 9 of the Japanese constitution is in the best interests of Japan. This matter is urgent, but before it is settled through <u>a national referendum</u>, there must be sufficient and <u>informed public discussion</u>. Yet, even then, can we be confident that the Japanese people will make the right decision?

Key terms

a national referendum 国民投票　　**informed public discussion** 正しい情報に基づいて公的議論や討論を行うこと

References

BBC Online. (2015, September 23). *Is Japan abandoning its pacifism?* BBC. Retrieved March 22, 2022 from https://www.bbc.com/news/world-asia-34278846

Global Firepower. (2022, January 12). 2022 Japan Military Strength. Retrieved March 22, 2022 from https://www.globalfirepower.com/country-military-strength-detail.php?country_id=japan

Ministry of Defense. (2021, April 9). *Joint Staff Press Release. Statistics on scrambles through FY2020.* Retrieved March 22, 2022 from https://www.mod.go.jp/js/Press/press2021/press_pdf/ p20210409_03.pdf

 Writing Task: Research and write about a controversial topic.

2つの意見に分かれる、政治的なトピックを選び、4つ、または、5つのパラグラフのエッセイを書きましょう。前の憲法9条の見本を見て、引用、参考文献まで入れてください。

A) 全体的な注意事項

1. 2つの意見とその理由を確認し、自分がどちらの立場で書くのかを明確にしておく。途中で、または、出だしと最後で意見が混ざらないように注意する。
2. 2つ、または、3つの理由とそれを支持するエビデンスや例を調べる。この際、それぞれの理由が、まったく違う側面の理由であることを確認する。

B) 書き方などの注意事項

1. I think, I believe、を多用しないで、「モノ」主語、it の形式主語、There is の英文を使うように心がける。
2. つなぎ言葉を使い、読み手に論理的に伝わるように書く。

Appendix

英文の中の数字
Letter 表記：one, two, three ...
Digit 表記：1, 2, 3 ...

Letter を使う場合
1. 1 から 9 までの数字は、Letter 表記にする。
   - ○　There are five candidates for the election.
   - ×　There are 5 candidates for the election.
2. 文章、タイトルの初めに数字が来る場合は、10 以上の数でも Letter 表記にする。
   - ○　Eighty-five people were infected today.
   - ×　85 people were infected today.
3. おおよその量を表す数字は Letter 表記にする。
   - ○　one fourth of the people

Digit を使う場合
1. 10 以上の数字は Digit 表記にする。
   - ○　There were 23 leaders captured in the region.
2. 小数点を含む数、またはパーセントや比率を表す数は、Digit 表記にする。
   - ○　The voting rate was 23.5%, rising by 1.4% from the previous election.
3. 年齢、金額、日付、単位の前などは1桁でも Digit 表記にする。
   - ○　3 years old　　4 dollars　　April 5　　6 centimeters
4. 統計学や数学的な場面で使用される数字は Digit 表記する。
   - ○　Multiplied by 3

Case by case
1. 世紀や10年（Decades）を表す時は、どちらでもよい。
   - ○　in the nineteenth century
   - ○　in the 19th century
2. 1つのセンテンスの中で、2つの数字が同じものを指す場合は、Letter または、Digit 表記を統一する。
   - ○　We asked for 5 sets, not 50.
   - ×　We asked for five sets, not 50.
3. 1つのセンテンスの中で、2つの数字が違うものを指す場合は、統一しなくてよい。
   - ○ That building has 12 rooms but one kitchen.
4. 大きな数字は Digit がベターだが、ただし統一する。
   - ○　Most women in that region earn from one million to five million dollars.
   - ×　Most women in that region earn from $1,000,000 to five million dollars.
5. 数字が連続するときは、片方を Digit で表記し、もう片方を Letter で表記する。
   - ○　There are three 5-year-old kids in the shelter.

引用・参考文献の書き方　How to Write Citations and References

The citations and references in this textbook follow the APA Style (7th edition).

A) Citations 本文の中に書く場合

1. Quoting

A direct quote is when you put the exact words of the author into your essay. Put the information in quotation marks, like this " ", and include the author's name, date of publication, and page number of the quote. **Examples**:

> … propaganda is the "smart way to keep people passive and obedient" (Chomsky, 2016, p. 234).
>
> … Chomsky (2016) wrote that propaganda is the "smart way to keep people passive and obedient" (p. 234).

2. Paraphrasing

Instead of writing long quotes, you can paraphrase the author in your own words. In this case, include the author's name and date of publication. **Examples**:

> One survey reported that more than 80% of LGBTQ+ employees are not out at work (au Jibun Bank, 2020).
>
> au Jibun Bank (2020) reported that more than 80% of LGBTQ+ employees are not out at work.

3. Secondary sources

If Author A (Markee, 2016) quotes Author B (Jones, 2013) and you did not read the original work by Author B, in your essay you should use the expression 'as cited in'. **Example**:

> … this often leads to conflict between rival economies (Jones, 2013, as cited in Markee, 2016).

In the references at the end, you should list Author A. **Example**:

> Markee, P. (2016). *International politics.* Cambridge University Press.

Note: Rather than rely on secondary sources, it is best to read the original work in order to confirm that the information is correct.

B) References（参考文献）としてエッセイの最後に書く場合

1. General rules

Below are some general rules for creating your reference list. For further details and information on other kinds of materials, refer to the APA Style (7th edition) website.

☐ Organize the reference list in alphabetical order. Indent the second line of each reference about five spaces. **Example**:

BBC Online. (2015, September 23). *Is Japan abandoning its pacifism?* BBC. https://www.bbc.com /news/world-asia-34278846

Gaimushō / MOFA. (2018, May 2). *SDGs NOW! 17 Goals to Transform Our World* [Video]. YouTube. https://www.youtube.com/watch?v=WXpZ-b4Qskg

Griffiths, M., O'Callaghan, T., & Roach, S. C. (2014). *International relations.* Routledge.

Suzuki, S. (2022, June 28). Calls made to strengthen state energy policies. *The Japan Times*, 3-4.

☐ For each reference in the list, you can name up to 20 authors. Use a comma and ampersand , & before the final author. **Example**:

Chauvin, L. O., Failola, A., & Dou, E. (2021, March 10). Poorer nations turn to China in scramble for vaccine supply. *The Japan News*, 12.

☐ When you reference multiple works by the same author, the earliest appears first in the list, followed by the most recent. If the works are published in the same year, letters are added after the year, starting with 'a'. **Example**:

Markee, P. (2016a). *International politics.* Cambridge University Press.

Markee, P. (2016b). *Changing politics in Japan.* Oxford University Press.

☐ When there is no date for the work, write (n.d.) in brackets, which means 'no date'.

2. Magazines, journals, etc.

Note: If you accessed an article online, you should include the URL.

Lastname, F. M. (year). Title of article. *Title of Magazine, (volume number)*issue number, pages. **Example**:

Mayer, E. (2021, August 16). Kids as young as four can now change gender in Scottish schools without parental consent. *Newsweek*, *30*(67), 69.

3. Books

Lastname, F. M. (year). Title of book. Name of Publisher. **Example**:

Griffiths, M., O'Callaghan, T., & Roach, S. C. (2014). *International relations.* Routledge.

4. Printed newspapers

Lastname, F. M. (year, Month, date). Title of article. Name of Newspaper, pages. **Example**:

Suzuki, S. (2022, June 28). Calls made to strengthen state energy policies. *The Japan Times*, 3-4.

5. Webpages

If an author's name appears on the webpage, write that name for your reference, not the website's name. If the author and website names are the same, you may omit the website's name. **Example**:

Gruberg, S., Mahowald, L., & Halpin, J. (2020, October 6). *The State of LGBTQ*

Community in 2020. The Center for American Progress. https://www.americanprogress.org/article/state-lgbtq-community-2020/

Note: **"Retrieved date, year from"** According to the APA (7th edition) rules, this phrase should only be included for websites that are updated on a regular basis, such as a social media profile. However, because we think this may happen with all online materials, for this textbook we have included the date we retrieved the material.

6. Online news
The format depends on whether the website also has a printed newspaper. If there is no newspaper, italicize only the article (like the example below). If there is a newspaper, italicize only the title of the newspaper. **Example**:

> BBC Online. (2015, September 23). *Is Japan abandoning its pacifism?* BBC. https://www.bbc.com/news/world-asia-34278846

7. YouTube or other online streaming
The person or organization who uploaded the video is considered the author. **Example**:

> Gaimushō / MOFA. (2018, May 2). *SDGs NOW! 17 Goals to Transform Our World* [Video]. YouTube. https://www.youtube.com/watch?v=WXpZ-b4Qskg

8. Twitter, Instagram, and Facebook posts
If the tweet or Instagram post includes videos, images, links to other sources, and so on, you should indicate that information in brackets after the content description. If possible, you should attempt to include emojis. The format is the same for Facebook posts, but need not include [@username].
Lastname, F. M. or Name of Organization [@username]. (year, Month date). *Content of the post up to the first 20 words* [Type of post]. Site Name. URL
Example:

> Truss, L. [@truszliz]. (2022, September 7). *As your Prime Minister, I am confident that together we can ride out the storm, rebuild our economy and become* [Tweet]. Twitter. https://twitter.com/trussliz/status/1567197484115496965

9. Materials written in Japanese
If you think readers might not be familiar with Japanese, you may write the title in romaji (in italics for book titles). You may also provide an English translation in square brackets [ ]. Author and publisher names may be written in romaji, too. A book would follow the format below:
Myouji, F.(year). *Romaji no taitoru [English translation]*. Name of Publisher.
Example:

> Ishida, H. (2019). *Hajimete manabu LGBT [The first lesson in LGBT]*. Natsume.

Additional Exercises

Exercise 次の文章に適切な言葉を下から選んで入れましょう。

Democracy and Autocracy

Many western countries and Japan have enjoyed democracy, but it is also true that some countries have experienced autocracy. Because ¹(   ) this, we can see that there are some advantages and disadvantages. Firstly, in a democracy, all citizens have power and an equal say about their lives, but in an

5 autocracy, one leader has the power to make decisions about people's lives. ²(   ) , in a democracy, citizens have freedom of thought and opinion and freedom of expression, and in an autocracy, one leader prohibits people ³(   ) expressing their opinion. Thirdly, in a democracy, since everyone can express their opinion freely, it takes a long time to make decisions. In an

10 autocracy, decisions can be made quickly because only the leader has to decide. ⁴(   ) , a democracy seems to come up ⁵(   ) good ideas for everyone because many people are involved. In an autocracy, if the leader is smart, the country will be led by good decisions, but if not, the opposite will happen. ⁶(   ) , both democracy and autocracy have advantages and disadvantages.

lastly	from	thus	of	secondly	with

Unit 4 | III | Writing Task

Question 5: アウトラインの空欄を埋めましょう。

| Outline |

I. One of the dangerous moments that could have led to WWIII — the Cuban Missile Crisis

A. On October 14

An American _____ discovered a _____ ballistic

missile being assembled in Cuba.

B. Reasons for Soviet missiles in Cuba

  1. The US and Cuba had a _____ relationship.

    a. _____ overthrew Batista's government that the US supported.

    b. The US imposed _____, and later launched a failed

    _____ on Cuba.

  2. The Soviets felt _____ about the US having nuclear weapons

  in _____.

II. The events leading to closure

A. On October 22

President _____ announced that the US would establish a blockade

around Cuba.

B. On October 24

The sea around Cuba was blocked to prevent the Soviets from _____

to Cuba.

C. On October 26

Khrushchev sent _____ to Kennedy.

D. On October 27

  1. A US plane was shot down over Cuba.

  2. Kennedy agreed _____ Cuba.

E. On October 28

Khrushchev agreed to _____ Soviet missiles from Cuba.

Exercise 3: Look at the map, and make at least four sentences to describe locations.

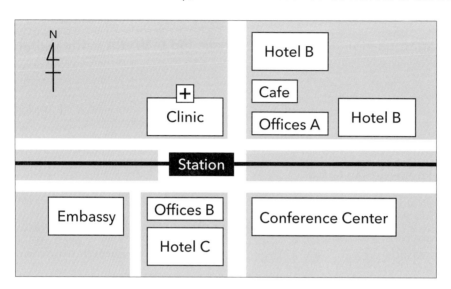

例：The embassy is to the left of Offices B.

1. _____

2. _____

3. _____

4. _____

| Unit 5 | IV | Grammar for Writing |

Exercise　次の文章に適切な副詞（句）のつなぎ言葉を選び空所に入れましょう。

Internationalization and Localization

　　Globalization is a new term emerging in the 21st century, but people and commodities moving across borders has occurred since ancient times. In terms of economic globalization, to be successful in business, people need to use the strategies of internationalization and localization. Internationalization 5 is the process in which products and services become widely available in different countries. Thus, internationalization is the process of promoting globalization, and enabling easy localization. [1](　　　　　）, customers can eat

122

McDonald's cheeseburgers or drive TOYOTA cars almost anywhere in the world. ²( ), this is not enough to compete with local businesses. Localization
10 is a necessary strategy to enable internationalization. Localization means that some products and services are changed to suit local taste and needs. ³( ), McDonald's in Japan offers teriyaki burgers as well as the cheeseburgers that are available in many countries. ⁴( ), they can increase their sales figures and have the power to compete both locally and internationally.
15 ⁵( ), globalization is made possible through the two processes of internationalization and localization.

| for instance | however | for example | in conclusion | as a result |

Exercise 次の文章に適切な分類の表現と前置詞・前置詞句を選び空所に入れましょう。答えが 1つではない場合もありますが、1つ入れればよいです。

Familiar UN Organizations

The United Nations (UN) is the largest organization dedicated to international peace and relations in the world. It has a variety of missions in many specific organizations, but the UN can be ¹( ) into six major divisions. Among them, the General Assembly, Security Council, and Economic and Social Council
5 are most familiar. The General Assembly is the division that makes decisions on UN policies. All member nations have one vote ²( ) their economic power and population. SDGs were adopted by this assembly. The Security Council is the division responsible ³( ) peace and security ⁴( ) the laws and policies. This division consists of five permanent-member countries
10 with veto power and 10 non-permanent member countries with two-year terms. The Economic and Social Council conducts surveys and research ⁵( ) international issues other than politics, such as women's rights and population. Since this council covers many areas, they set up committees and cooperate with specialized agencies such as UNESCO. ⁶( ) the nature of these activities,
15 many kinds of people are involved. In summary, the UN can be ⁷( ) into six major divisions, three of which are very familiar.

| on | divided | due to | regardless of | under | for | classified |

Question 3: What similarities and differences are in this essay? Fill in the blanks.

	Japan	The US
Similarities	1. LGBTQ+ people tend to hide their sexual identities 2.	The same experiences
Differences		1. Same-sex marriage is admitted by law.

Unit 8 　IV 　Grammar for Writing

Exercise 　次の文章に適切な語句を選び空所に入れましょう。

Living as LGBTQ+ in Japan and the US

　　There are similarities and differences in the LGBTQ+ experiences of Japan and the US. Although LGBTQ+ progress in Japan lags far behind, LGBTQ+ people in the US still experience discrimination. Namely, LGBTQ+ people in

¹(   ) countries tend to hide their sexual identities to avoid discrimination. ²(   ) an American think tank survey in 2020, 54% of LGBTQ+ people hid their personal relationships. Another survey conducted the same year by au Jibun Bank Corp. ³(   ) that more than 80% of Japanese LGBTQ+ employees were not "out" at work. Furthermore, in ⁴(   ) countries, transgender people have difficulty using public restrooms. However, there are more fundamental differences for LGBTQ+ people living in Japan and the US For example, since 2015, same-sex marriage has been legal in the US. The US Supreme Court made this decision and ordered all states to follow the law. That same year more than 390,000 couples were married. ⁵(   ), there is no law allowing same-sex marriage in Japan. Instead, in 2015, Setagaya and Shibuya wards established a partnership system. This allows same-sex couples to apply together for public rental housing and be recognized as family members at hospitals. However, same-sex partners in Japan have no right of inheritance or tax benefits. ⁶(   ) the US, only about 1,300 same-sex couples were joined in 2020. Thus, there are similarities and differences regarding LGBTQ+ people living in Japan and the US.

| found | both | both | unlike | on the other hand | according to |

Unit 9 III Writing Task

Question 3: 次の表を埋めて、エッセイの構造を明確にしましょう。

Points	The US	Japan
Political Empowerment		
Economic Participation and Opportunity		

Exercise どちらか適切な語句を選びましょう。

Contrasting the Gender Gap between the US and Japan

In the 2021 Global Gender Gap Report, both the US and Japan rank lower than some other democratic and economic countries. Yet, the contrasts in the two countries' ranks show how different their situations really are. In terms of political empowerment, the US ranks 37th at 0.329, [1](**but** / **unlike**) Japan ranks 147th at 0.061.
5 Additionally, the percentage of female members in the US Congress was about 30%, [2](**however** / **while**) only 9.9% in the Japanese Diet. The main obstacle for women to become members of Congress is said to be the US election system. [3](**Unlike** / **By contrast**), lack of specialist knowledge and the difficulty of balancing housework and childcare are the reasons in Japan. In terms of economic participation and
10 opportunity, the US ranks only 30th at 0.75, [4](**higher than** / **whereas**) Japan ranks 120th at 0.6%. Other research shows that Japanese men work the longest hours among the 34 OECD countries, [5](**in contrast** / **although**) to men in the US which ranks 16th. It makes sense then, that Japanese women rank third for time spent doing housework, which is almost five times that of Japanese men. Research by
15 a Japanese kitchen maker, [6](**however** / **yet**), found that men in the US spend the most time doing housework compared to those in Japan, South Korea, Germany, and Denmark.

Exercise　下から適切な語句を選び入れましょう。

The Taliban in Afghanistan

There are many aspects of terrorism. This is an analysis of the Taliban in Afghanistan, from the perspectives of religion and ethno-nationalism. As an organization, the Taliban was one of the most extreme and destructive who followed a fundamentalist, religious ideology. It was a group that
5 ¹( ) believed in traditional Islamic law. The group emerged from the Afghan War with the former Soviet Union between 1978 and 1992. They had taken the capital city, Kabul, by 1996 and were in control of most of the country ²( ). However, they faced severe resistance from ethnic and other groups due to their strict religious ideology. While fighting against the US and NATO
10 forces at the beginning of the 21st century, the Taliban's motivations can also be classified as ethno-nationalistic. After the 9/11 attacks on the US in 2001, the US started a war in Afghanistan to kill Osama bin Laden, the leader of Al Qaeda, and prevent the Taliban from protecting him. During the conflict, resistance against US-led forces increased ³( ) and encouraged people to join both the
15 Taliban and Al Qaeda, not because of Islamic fundamentalist ideology, but because of anti-US sentiment. As a result, with the support of the general public, a large number of Taliban soldiers covered most of the country so that they could fight ⁴( ). In conclusion, the various motivations of terrorism can often overlap, depending on the circumstances. The Taliban was ⁵( ) a fundamentalist
20 group, but later adopted ethno-nationalism to fight against foreign influences. Some have considered the recent revival of the Taliban as a 'a global failure' of the western world. In any case, if the Taliban's goal is to create a new, sovereign-state system, it will be difficult for them to remain terrorists.

gradually	initially	strictly	advantageously	eventually

Exercise 下から適切な語句を選び入れましょう。

Poverty in Niger

The Republic of Niger is a very poor country. There are three main reasons for this situation. The first is a high birth rate. The World Data Atlas states that the birth rate in 2020 was 6.7 births per woman, and the rate of increase was 3.8%. [1]( ), it was predicted that the country might experience a population

5 explosion. [2]( ) that, it was very difficult to support and educate families. [3]( ), the literacy rate was very low as well, making it difficult for people to break the vicious cycle of poverty. The second reason is seasonal droughts. These droughts [4]( ) in the desertification and devastation of farmlands. Consequently, this [5]( ) to a shortage of both food and drinking water,

10 along with malnutrition and the spread of disease. It was very difficult to solve this problem [6]( ) water storage and transport systems were old and in need of repair. Additionally, when people moved in search of new land, they experienced conflict with locals in the new areas. The third reason is an unstable government. Food shortages have [7]( ) a wide gap between the rich and the poor, which

15 upsets the overall stability of the country. The Nigerian government has experienced military coups many times, and the spread of poverty not only encourages terrorist activity but also disrupts economic development. [8]( ), a high birth rate, seasonal droughts, and an unstable government are responsible for poverty and other problems in the Republic of Niger. Although these problems may seem far

20 away from our daily lives, as fellow humans we have a duty to help. If we don't, the situation will only get worse and eventually affect the global economy and other countries too.

resulted	because of	led	because	therefore	thus
as a result	created				

Exercise 下から選んで適切な語句を入れましょう。答えが1つではない場合もありますが、1つ入れればよいです。

The Destruction of Forests

　　Forests all around the world have been rapidly disappearing. [1](　　　　), all this deforestation has had some major negative effects. The first is global warming. Trees, along with other plants, absorb CO_2 and produce oxygen. [2](　　　　), if the number of trees is reduced the amount of CO_2 increases. This
5　means heat won't be released from the earth, and temperatures will [3](　　　　) rise. The second negative effect is that deforestation increases the possibility of floods and landslides. If a mountain has no trees, you can probably imagine what catastrophes heavy rains could cause. [4](　　　　), in 2021, many cyclones and hurricanes created floods and landslides, damaging huge areas in places all over
10　the world. The third effect is that deforestation creates a gap between the rich and the poor. This causes many people to suffer from starvation and poverty. In some developing countries, many people depend on edible plants for food such as nuts and mushrooms, and use trees as fuel for fire. To make matters worse, some of these countries have experienced a population explosion. [5](　　　　), many more
15　trees are needed to supply this growing demand. [6](　　　　), deforestation leads to three major negative effects: global warming, floods and landslides, and a gap between the rich and the poor. We should all remember that forests are essential for our lives, and work on establishing ways to ensure they will always exist.

| as a result | thus | as it turned out | consequently |
| therefore | inevitably | | |

Question 2: 日米の貿易問題と、その解決策を表に書きましょう。

	Japan	The U.S.
Problem 1: Cars		
Solutions		
Problem 2: Agricultural products		
Solutions		

Exercise　下から適切な語句を選び入れましょう。

Trade Issues Between Japan and the US

　　There were two major trade ¹( ) between Japan and the US, even after the Japan-US Trade Agreement ²( ) in 2020. The first issue was automobiles. For the US, the imbalance of exports and imports was large, with 80% of the US trade deficit caused by automobiles. To protect their automobile

5　industry, the US ³( ) customs duties for passenger cars, trucks, and car parts. On the other hand, Japan did not impose any tariffs on American automobiles, so Japan demanded that the US eliminate tariffs on passenger cars. However, out of fear that the US might limit the quota of imports, Japan agreed to the 2.5% tariffs. In the bilateral agreement and TPP, tariffs were supposed to

10　be eliminated, but negotiations stopped when the US left the TPP. The second issue was agricultural products. Both countries had special reasons for protecting their farmers and agricultural industries. In the US, midwestern agricultural states were important for the presidential election, and after leaving the TPP, they had to compete with EU and TPP members in the Japanese market. In Japan, importing

15　more agricultural products might decrease the country's food self-sufficiency rate, and in terms of production costs, Japan was at a disadvantage because the US ⁴( ) large-scale farming systems to provide lower prices than Japan. Because of this, Japan ⁵( ) several measures, such as reducing production costs, increasing product quality, and providing subsidies to small and medium-

20　sized livestock farmers. Thus, both countries shared two major trade issues, but needed to compromise through tough negotiations, all the while following the rules of the WTO for ⁶( ) the benefits of free trade.

imposed	took	utilized	concluded	enjoying	issues

著者
Paul Underwood（ポール・アンダーウッド）
仲谷　都（なかや　みやこ）

CLIL国際関係で英語ライティング

2023年 2 月20日　第 1 版発行

著　　者——Paul Underwood
　　　　　　仲谷　都
発 行 者——前田俊秀
発 行 所——株式会社 三修社
　　　　　　〒150-0001東京都渋谷区神宮前 2-2-22
　　　　　　TEL03-3405-4511　FAX03-3405-4522
　　　　　　振替 00190-9-72758
　　　　　　https://www.sanshusha.co.jp
　　　　　　編集担当　菊池　暁
印刷・製本——壮光舎印刷株式会社

©2023 Printed in Japan　ISBN978-4-384-33525-5 C1082
表紙デザイン——Izumiya（岩泉卓屋）
本文DTP————川原田良一
音声録音————ELEC
音声製作————高速録音株式会社
音声吹込————Chris Koprowski

教科書準拠CD発売
本書の準拠CDをご希望の方は弊社までお問い合わせください。